33 Day Consecration to Jesus Through Mary

Inspired by St. Louis Marie de Montfort

Published by

Morning Star Publications
The Presbytery,
Gowel,
Carrick on Shannon, County Leitrim,
Ireland

ISBN 978-0-9567021-5-9

Print Management by
Transform Management Ltd
info@1025transform.co.uk

Printed and bound in the UK

Introduction

St Louis de Montfort in his 33-day consecration (Total Consecration to Jesus through Mary) helps us to consecrate our hearts and all that we have in our lives to the Immaculate Heart of Mary, and through her heart to the Most Sacred Heart of Jesus.

This devotion has helped me to understand a love and a depth of Mary and Jesus that I didn't think was possible. There is a supernatural grace in this consecration that I feel is beyond human words or understanding. The late Holy Father St. John Paul II stated that through reading this consecration his life was transformed he said "this Marian devotion has since remained an integral part of my interior life and of my spiritual theology"

I believe that this devotion is truly life changing and brings us to a deep foundation built on the rock of Christ. It protects us in this world of spiritual warfare and helps us to understand our gifts given by God the creator.

I would advise that before starting this devotion you would pray for the grace of perseverance and give it your fullest attention and time, because in spiritual warfare the enemy will try everything to rob you of these incredible graces. The protection prayer on page 3 is a good prayer to pray each day of this devotion.

Each day will consist of an opening prayer, scripture reading, a reading from the writings of St. Louis de Montfort, a reflection and various prayers. It is recommended that you finish this devotion on a Marian feast day, so before you start, check the calendar of possible consecration dates for the best day to begin.

St Louis de Montfort speaks of a remnant Marian army that will bring immeasurable graces to heaven and I believe as St Louis de Montfort did that this consecration is the commissioning to that army and I cannot recommend it highly enough.

John Pridmore

Contents

Calendar of possible consecration dates

Start Date	Marian Feast Day on which you will finish on	Consecration Date
29 Nov	Mary Mother of God	1 Jan
6 Dec	Our Lady of Prompt Succor	8 Jan
19 Dec	Our Lady of Consolation	21 Jan
21 Dec	Espousal of the Virgin Mary	23 Jan
22 Dec	Our Lady of Tears	24 Jan
31 Dec	Presentation of the Lord	2 Feb
9 Jan	Our Lady of Lourdes	11 Feb
20 Feb	Annunciation	25 Mar
24 Mar	Our Lady of Good Counsel	26 Apr
26 Mar	Feast of St. Louis de Montfort	28 Apr
10 Apr	Our Lady of Fatima	13 May
21 Apr	Our Lady Help of Christians	24 May
28 Apr	Visitation	31 May
7 May	Our Lady Virgin Mother of Grace	9 Jun
25 May	Our Mother of Perpetual Help	27 Jun
30 May	Visitation by Mary to Elizabeth	2 Jul
13 Jun	Our Lady of Mount Carmel	16 Jul
15 Jun	Humility of the Blessed Virgin Mary	17 Jul
30 Jun	Our Lady of the Angels	2 Aug
4 Jul	Our Lady of the Snow	5 Aug
11 Jul	Our Lady, Refuge of Sinners	13 Aug
13 Jul	Assumption	15 Aug
19 Jul	Our Lady of Knock	21 Aug
20 Jul	Queenship of Mary	22 Aug
6 Aug	Birth of Mary	8 Sep
10 Aug	The Most Holy Name of Mary	12 Sep
13 Aug	Our Lady of Sorrows	15 Sep
22 Aug	Our Lady of Mercy	24 Sep
29 Aug	Holy Protection of the Mother of God	1 Oct
2 Sep	Our Lady of the Rosary	7 Oct
5 Sep	Our Lady of Good Remedy	8 Oct
8 Sep	Maternity of the Blessed Virgin Mary	11 Oct
13 Sep	Purity of the Blessed Virgin Mary	16 Oct
19 Oct	Presentation of the Blessed Virgin Mary	21 Nov
5 Nov	Immaculate Conception	8 Dec
9 Nov	Our Lady of Guadalupe	12 Dec
16 Nov	Expectation of the Blessed Virgin Mary	18 Dec

Healing and Protection prayer

Heavenly Father, I praise and thank You for all You have given me. Please cover me with the protective, precious blood of Your Son Jesus Christ. Increase Your Holy Spirit in me with His gifts of wisdom, knowledge, understanding, hunger for prayer, guidance and discernment to help me know Your will and surrender to it more completely.

Father, Please heal my negative emotions and any wounds in my heart and spirit. Send the sword of Your Holy Spirit to sever and break all spells, curses, hexes, voodoo and all negative genetic, intergenerational and addictive material, past, present or to come, known or unknown, against me, my relationships and family, finances, possessions and ministry.

Father, I forgive and I ask forgiveness for my sins and failings, and I ask that my whole person, body and mind, heart and will, soul and spirit, memory and emotions, attitudes and values lie cleansed, renewed and protected by the most precious blood of Your Son, Jesus.

In the name, power, blood and authority of Jesus Christ I bind and break the power and effect in or around me of any and all evil spirits who are trying to harm me in any way, and I command these spirits and their companion spirits in the name of the Father, the Son, and the Holy Spirit to leave me peacefully and quietly and go immediately and directly to the Eucharistic presence of Jesus Christ in the closest Catholic Church tabernacle to be disposed of by Jesus and never again return to harm me.

Dear Holy Spirit, please fill up any void in me to overflowing with your great love. All this Father I pray in the name of Jesus Christ by the guidance of Your Holy Spirit. Immaculate heart of Mary spouse of the Holy Spirit, please pray for and with me.

Amen

St. Louis de Montfort writes, "Those who desire to take up this devotion should spend at least twelve days emptying themselves of the spirit of the world, which is opposed to the Spirit of Jesus'

These coming days we will undertake to rid ourselves of the spirit of the world by prayer, fasting and almsgiving. For the rest of our lives we will battle against this spirit that prevails in our modern culture and society to put on the Spirit of Christ in which we were baptised.

St. Louis de Montfort teaches that through self-denial we can find power to overcome and renounce the spirit of the world. By putting ourselves last we are enabled to put God and others first. And by doing so, help root out our preoccupation with self, materialistic values, pride and vanities. These twelve days help mould us into having a love of God's commandments and obedience to His will in our lives. It brings us out of the darkness of mind and spirit, seduction and corruption, to a light, freedom and clarity of the Holy Spirit.

Theme : Trusting in God and His Providence

Opening Prayer

Come Holy Spirit, come by means of the powerful intercession of the Immaculate Heart of Mary your well beloved spouse (3 times)

Scripture

Matthew 6:25-34

Jesus said 'That is why I am telling you not to worry about your life and what you are to eat, nor about your body and what you are to wear. Surely life is more than food, and the body more than clothing! Look at the birds in the sky. They do not sow or reap or gather into barns; yet your heavenly Father feeds them. Are you not worth much more than they are? Can any of you, however much you worry, add one single cubit to your span of life? And why worry about clothing? Think of the flowers growing in the fields; they never have to work or spin, yet I assure you that not even Solomon in all his royal robes was clothed like one of these. Now if that is how God clothes the wild flowers growing in the field which are there today and thrown into the furnace tomorrow, will he not much more look after you, you who have so little faith? So do not worry; do not say, "What are we to eat? What are we to drink? What are we to wear?" It is the gentiles who set their hearts on all these things. Your heavenly Father knows you need them all. Set your hearts on His kingdom first, and on God's saving justice, and all these other things will be given you as well. So, do not worry about tomorrow: tomorrow will take care of itself. Each day has enough trouble of its own.'

The grace of God is absolutely necessary

Chosen soul, living image of God and redeemed by the precious blood of Jesus Christ, God wants you to become holy like Him in this life, and glorious like Him in the next. It is certain that growth in the holiness of God is your vocation. All your thoughts, words, actions, everything you suffer or undertake must lead you towards that end.
Dust into light, uncleanness into purity, sinfulness into holiness, creature into Creator, man into God! A marvellous work, I repeat, so difficult in itself, and even impossible for a mere creature to bring about, for only God can accomplish it by giving His grace abundantly and in an extraordinary manner. The very creation of the universe is not as great an achievement as this.

Reflection

In my own life I have found that in trusting God and opening my heart to His providence, He is a God who is never outdone with His generosity. The more I have learned to give and not hold anything back, the more it seems to give God permission to pour out an abundance of grace and blessings in my everyday life. We cannot be too generous.

"It is not enough to give, we are called to give until it hurts". (Blessed Mother Teresa)

Resolution

As we begin this period of preparation it is necessary for us to decide how much time we will put aside each day to commit to personal prayer and reflection. This must be a commitment we intend to keep for the entire 33 days.

Let us ask the Blessed Virgin Mary for the grace to be generous as God is generous.

Recite prayers for the day *Veni Creator, Ave Maris Stella, Magnificat,* (Pages 30-32)

Theme : God is the Foundation of our lives

Opening Prayer

Come Holy Spirit, come by means of the powerful intercession of the Immaculate Heart of Mary your well beloved spouse (3 times)

Scripture

Matthew 7:24

Jesus said 'Therefore, everyone who listens to these words of mine and acts on them will be like a sensible man who built his house on rock.'

St. Louis De Montfort Reading for today
From the Secret of Mary (Reference #4)

Chosen soul, how will you bring this about? What steps will you take to reach the high level to which God is calling you? The means of holiness and salvation are known to everybody, since they are found in the gospel; the masters of the spiritual life have explained them; the saints have practiced them and shown how essential they are for those who wish to be saved and attain perfection. These means are: sincere humility, unceasing prayer, complete self-denial, abandonment to divine Providence, and obedience to the will of God.

Reflection

Personal prayer is where we bore into the rock of Jesus and plant our roots firmly in God's foundation and there is no substitute. The more we pray the more we give God permission to bless our lives.

"Give God permission". (Blessed Mother Teresa)

Resolution

Ask Our Lady for a deep desire to rid ourselves of all attachments that hold us back from a closer relationship with God and to commit to more personal prayer time.

Recite prayers for the day *Veni Creator, Ave Maris Stella, Magnificat* (Pages 30-32)

Theme : Jesus Christ was born into poverty for my sake, so that I could be redeemed from my brokenness and sins.

Opening Prayer

Come Holy Spirit, come by means of the powerful intercession of the Immaculate Heart of Mary your well beloved spouse (3 times)

Scripture

Mark 10:28-30

Peter said. 'We have left everything and followed you. 'Jesus said, 'In truth I tell you, there is no one who has left house, brothers, sisters, mother, father, children or land for my sake and for the sake of the gospel who will not receive a hundred times as much, houses, brothers, sisters, mothers, children and land and persecutions too now in this present time and, in the world to come, eternal life.'

St. Louis De Montfort Reading for today
From Love of Eternal Wisdom (Reference #194)

The Necessity of Mortification

The Holy Spirit tells us that Wisdom is not found in the hearts of those who live in comfort, (Job 28.13) gratifying their passions and bodily desires, because "they who are of the flesh cannot please God," and "the wisdom of the flesh is an enemy to God." (Rom 8.8,7) All those who belong to Christ, incarnate Wisdom, have crucified their flesh with its passions and desires. They always bear about in their bodies the dying of Jesus. They continually carry their cross daily. They are dead and indeed buried with Christ. (Gal 5.24; 2 Cor 4.10; Lk 9.23; Rom 6.4,8) These words of the Holy Spirit show us more clearly than the light of day that, if we are to possess incarnate Wisdom, Jesus Christ, we must practice self-denial and renounce the world and self.

Reflection

When we sacrifice we open a door to the possibility of God's miracles and the more we sacrifice the bigger that door becomes. The more I have learned to give God in these areas of mortification the more miracles I have witnessed in God changing situations or peoples lives. A priest friend of mine once stated that fasting is a grace completely on its own and there is no good works or prayer that can replace it.

"The two mortifications that God can never refuse are fasting from food and fasting from sleep." (St. John Vianney)

Resolution

Ask our Blessed Mother for the grace to renounce some comfort and make sacrifices for the sake of the Kingdom of God.

Recite prayers for the day *Veni Creator, Ave Maris Stella, Magnificat* (Pages 30-32)

Theme : Making time for God

Opening Prayer

Come Holy Spirit, come by means of the powerful intercession of the Immaculate Heart of Mary your well beloved spouse (3 times)

Scripture

Matthew 6:5-6

Jesus said 'and when you pray, do not imitate the hypocrites: they love to say their prayers standing up in the synagogues and at the street corners for people to see them. In truth I tell you, they have had their reward. But when you pray, go to your private room, shut yourself in, and so pray to your Father who is in that secret place, and your Father who sees all that is done in secret will reward you.

St. Louis De Montfort Reading for today
From Secret of the Rosary

Wondrous to relate, this divine Wisdom chose to leave the bosom of His Father and enter the womb of a virgin and there repose amid the lilies of her purity. Desiring to give Himself to her by becoming man in her, He sent the archangel Gabriel to greet her on His behalf and to declare to her that she had won His heart and He would become man within her if she gave her consent. The archangel fulfilled his mission and assured her that she would still remain a virgin while becoming a mother. Notwithstanding her desire to be lowly, Mary wholeheartedly gave the angel that priceless consent which the Blessed Trinity, all the angels and the whole world awaited for so many centuries. Humbling herself before her Creator she said" "Behold the handmaid of the Lord. Let it be done to me according to your word"

Reflection

Do you want to know what God wants? He wants your everything! He wants us to give Him permission to run our lives in every area. When we find the pearl of great price, which is the love of God for us, we should be willing to exchange everything for that pearl. In my life there were many areas where I wanted to be in control as this kept me under the illusion of being secure, but the reality was that in all these areas where I was controlling, I was a prisoner. The more I have learned to allow God to be in control and to trust Him the more free I have become and the freedom that God offers us is a taste of heaven on earth.

"I want you to be happy, always happy, I repeat what I want is your happiness." Phillipians 4:4

Resolution

Ask Our Lady for the grace to surrender to God's will in all things.

Recite prayers for the day *Veni Creator, Ave Maris Stella, Magnificat* (Pages 30-32)

Theme : Our prayers should not be self seeking but lead us to say 'Thy will be done'

Opening Prayer

Come Holy Spirit, come by means of the powerful intercession of the Immaculate Heart of Mary your well beloved spouse (3 times)

Scripture

Matthew 6:9-13

Jesus said ' so you should pray like this: Our Father in heaven, may your name be held holy, your kingdom come, your will be done, on earth as in heaven. Give us today our daily bread. And forgive us our debts, as we have forgiven those who are in debt to us. And do not put us to the test, but save us from the evil one.'

St. Louis De Montfort Reading for today
From Love of Eternal Wisdom (Reference #10.2)

Nothing is more consoling than to know divine Wisdom. Happy are those who listen to Him; happier still are those who desire Him and seek Him; but happiest of all are those who keep His laws. Their hearts will be filled with that infinite consolation which is the joy and happiness of the eternal Father and the glory of the angels (cf. Prov. 2:1-9). If only we knew the joy of a soul that perceives the beauty of divine Wisdom and is nourished with the milk of divine kindness, we would cry out with the bride in the Song of Songs: "Your love is better than wine" (Song 1:3) better by far than all created delights. This is especially true when divine Wisdom says to those who contemplate Him, "Taste and see" (Ps. 33:9) eat and drink, be filled with my eternal sweetness (Song 5:1), for you will discover that conversing with me is in no way distasteful, that my companionship is never tedious and in me only will you find joy and contentment (Wisd. 8:16).

Reflection

I remember there was a time when I was praying for the members of my family to be blessed by God and a person said to me "God has heard your prayers about your family" and I found myself reflecting on what God wanted me to pray for. This helped me open my heart to a depth of prayer that I didn't know existed. This realm which is "Thy will be done" is a deep gift where we become God's instrument in speaking the desires of God's heart and praying for those desires. When we praise God it is a completely selfless act.

"When we sing, we pray twice." (St Augustine)

Resolution

Ask our Blessed Mother that we would pray as God would want.

Recite prayers for the day *Veni Creator, Ave Maris Stella, Magnificat* (Pages 30-32)

Day 6 Renouncing the Spirit of the World

Theme : Jesus took the path of self-sacrifice to show us the way.

Opening Prayer

Come Holy Spirit, come by means of the powerful intercession of the Immaculate Heart of Mary your well beloved spouse (3 times)

Scripture

Luke 9:22-25

Then, speaking to all, He said, 'If anyone wants to be a follower of mine, let him renounce himself and take up his cross every day and follow me. Anyone who wants to save his life will lose it; but anyone who loses his life for my sake, will save it. What benefit is it to anyone to win the whole world and forfeit or lose his very self?"

St. Louis De Montfort Reading for today
From Friends of the Cross (Reference #7)

My dear brothers and sisters, there are two companies that appear before you each day: the followers of Christ and the followers of the world. Our dear Saviour's company is on the right, climbing up a narrow road, made all the narrower by the world's immorality. Our Master leads the way, barefooted, crowned with thorns, covered with blood, and laden with a heavy cross. Those who follow Him, though most valiant are only a handful, either because His quiet voice is not heard amid the tumult of the world, or because people lack the courage to follow Him in His poverty, sufferings, humiliations and other crosses which His servants must carry all the days of their life. Do you listen to the voice of Jesus who, burdened with His Cross, calls out to you, "Come after me; anyone who follows me will not be walking in the dark; be brave; I have conquered the world."

Reflection

Many times in my life I wanted to plan when and what I should be doing and normally have made a great mess of these situations. The more I have learned to seek God's will in who and what He created me to be, and where and when He wanted me to go, the more these situations have all fallen into place like a giant divine jigsaw. If someone had said to me what God could do in just a few years to give me a deep freedom and abandonment to His will, I would not have believed them. But God in His patience, mercy and divine wonder has slowly brought me to this grace and when I look back at these years I see how God's plan is so perfect and every detail is so necessary for His divine tapestry.

"When you were young you went where you liked, but when you grow older I will place a belt around your waist and lead you where you would rather not go." John 21:18

Resolution

Ask our Blessed Mother for the grace to not be afraid of the cross but to embrace it as her Son did.

Recite prayers for the day *Veni Creator, Ave Maris Stella, Magnificat* (Pages 30-32)

Theme : Repentance and Conversion

Opening Prayer

Come Holy Spirit, come by means of the powerful intercession of the Immaculate Heart of Mary your well beloved spouse (3 times)

Scripture

Luke 15:4-7

Jesus said 'Which one of you with a hundred sheep, if he lost one, would fail to leave the ninety-nine in the desert and go after the missing one till he found it? And when he found it, would he not joyfully take it on his shoulders and then, when he got home, call together his friends and neighbours, saying to them, "Rejoice with me, I have found my sheep that was lost." In the same way, I tell you, there will be more rejoicing in heaven over one sinner repenting than over ninety-nine upright people who have no need of repentance."

St. Louis De Montfort Reading for today
From Secret of the Rosary (Reference #23)

The Gospel teaches us that a sinner who is converted and who does penance gives joy to all the angels. If the repentance and conversion of one sinner is enough to make the angels rejoice, how great must be the happiness and jubilation of the whole heavenly court and what glory for our Blessed Lord Himself to see us here on earth meditating devoutly and lovingly on His humiliations and torments and on His cruel and shameful death! Let us meditate, then, on the life and sufferings of our Saviour by means of the holy Rosary; let us learn to know Him well and to be grateful for all His blessings, so that, on the Day of Judgment, He may number us among His children and His friends.

Reflection

"Go in peace your sins are forgiven you". I have often heard these words in my life since I've been walking with Jesus and yet they are words that I never seem to take for granted but always have a massive effect on my life, as a broken sinner who is being redeemed by the blood and torn body of my friend and saviour Jesus. Each time I go to confession I receive the graces to know the love of God for me. I believe that every time we taste this sacrament in honesty and sincerity we renew our personal friendship and relationship with God's divine son.

"Sooner would heaven and earth fade away than anyone asking for my mercy be turned away." (Jesus to St Faustina)

Resolution

Make time for an examination of conscience and make a commitment to attend the Sacrament of Confession with an open and sincere heart.

Recite prayers for the day *Veni Creator, Ave Maris Stella, Magnificat* (Pages 30-32)

Theme : Depend upon Christ and don't be tied down by worldly success or esteem

Opening Prayer

Come Holy Spirit, come by means of the powerful intercession of the Immaculate Heart of Mary your well beloved spouse (3 times)

Scripture

Matthew 19:16-22

And now a man came to Him and asked, 'Master, what good deed must I do to possess eternal life?' Jesus said to him, 'Why do you ask me about what is good? There is one alone who is good. But if you wish to enter into life, keep the commandments.' He said, 'Which ones?' Jesus replied, 'these: You shall not kill. You shall not commit adultery. You shall not steal. You shall not give false witness. Honour your father and your mother. You shall love your neighbour as yourself.' The young man said to Him, 'I have kept all these. What more do I need to do?' Jesus said, 'If you wish to be perfect, go and sell your possessions and give the money to the poor, and you will have treasure in heaven; then come, follow me.' But when the young man heard these words he went away sad, for he was a man of great wealth.

St. Louis De Montfort Reading for today
From True devotion to Mary (Reference #135)

If we can conceive on earth no employment more lofty than the service of God - if the least servant of God is richer, more powerful and more noble than all the kings and emperors of this earth, unless they also are the servants of God - what must be the riches, the power and the dignity of the faithful and perfect servant of God, who is devoted to His service entirely and without reserve, to the utmost extent possible?

Such is the faithful and loving slave of Jesus in Mary who has given Himself up entirely to the service of that King of Kings, by the hands of His holy Mother, and has reserved nothing for Himself. Not all the gold of earth nor all the beauties of the heavens can repay Him.

Reflection

At the beginning of my journey with God I had a lot of wealth and possessions, at that time I had a desire in my heart like St Francis of Assisi to give away everything and follow Christ. After attempting this many times I was always brought back to the same place, a little poorer and a little wiser, until God asked me to give up everything and to come follow Him. Sometimes the overwhelming desire in our hearts is to give God everything and to walk away from this world of possessions and materialism. I think that desire is what God craves for, but we should always wait for Him to call us to a life of poverty and not force that desire upon ourselves. We can live with Christ in the world, but not be part of the world. We can have materialistic wealth and possessions and they are not a blockage to God's grace, as long as we know they are on loan to us from God and have no hold over us.

"If you are born in poverty, embrace your poverty. If you are born in immense wealth embrace that position. But always surrender to the will of God and be generous." (Blessed Mother Teresa)

Resolution

Ask Our Lady for the grace to be generous in our response to God's call.

Recite prayers for the day, *Veni Creator, Ave Maris Stella, Magnificat* (Pages 30-32)

Theme: Seeking to live a Godly life

Opening Prayer

Come Holy Spirit, come by means of the powerful intercession of the Immaculate Heart of Mary your well beloved spouse (3 times)

Scripture

Matthew: 5:2-12

Then He began to speak. This is what He taught them: How blessed are the poor in spirit: the kingdom of Heaven is theirs. Blessed are the gentle: they shall have the earth as inheritance. Blessed are those who mourn: they shall be comforted. Blessed are those who hunger and thirst for uprightness: they shall have their fill. Blessed are the merciful: they shall have mercy shown them. Blessed are the pure in heart: they shall see God. Blessed are the peacemakers: they shall be recognised as children of God. Blessed are those who are persecuted in the cause of uprightness: the kingdom of Heaven is theirs. 'Blessed are you when people abuse you and persecute you and speak all kinds of calumny against you falsely on my account. Rejoice and be glad, for your reward will be great in heaven; this is how they persecuted the prophets before you.

St. Louis De Montfort Reading for today
True Devotion (Reference #89)

It is difficult to persevere in holiness because of the excessively corrupting influence of the world. The world is so corrupt that it seems almost inevitable that religious hearts be soiled, if not by its mud, at least by its dust. It is something of a miracle for anyone to stand firm in the midst of this raging torrent and not be swept away, to weather this stormy sea and not be drowned, or robbed by pirates; to breathe this pestilential air and not be contaminated by it. It is Mary, the singularly faithful Virgin over whom Satan had never any power, who works this miracle for those who truly love her.

Reflection

When I was in Thailand there was a lot of promiscuity on view and this impurity was starting to affect my peace. I remember emailing an enclosed Carmelite nun and saying to her how I craved to have a pure heart. Her reply was so uplifting and helpful as she said, "That it is that desire of purity, it is that desire of holiness, it is that desire of selflessness that blesses God's heart. We do not have to succeed, but we do have to try, and the more we try the more we make God happy.

"God does not ask for success, only faithfulness."
(Blessed Mother Teresa)

Resolution

Let us implore Our Lady's help to try and seek Gods kingdom with all our hearts.

Recite prayers for the day, *Veni Creator, Ave Maris Stella, Magnificat* (Pages 30-32)

Day 10 Renouncing the Spirit of the World

Theme: We serve God first.

Opening Prayer

Come Holy Spirit, come by means of the powerful intercession of the Immaculate Heart of Mary your well beloved spouse (3 times)

Scripture

Matthew 22:34-40

But when the Pharisees heard that He had silenced the Sadducees with his reply, they met together to question Him again. One of them, an expert in religious law, tried to trap Him with this question: "Teacher, which is the most important commandment in the Law of Moses?"

Jesus replied, "You must love the Lord your God with all your heart, all your soul, and all your mind. This is the first and greatest commandment. A second is equally important: Love your neighbour as yourself. The entire law and all the demands of the prophets are based on these two commandments."

St. Louis de Montfort Reading for today
From True Devotion (Reference #178)

Oh! How happy is the man who has given everything to Mary, and has trusted Himself to Mary in everything and for everything! He belongs all to Mary, and Mary belongs all to Him. He can say boldly with David, "Mary is made for me;" or with the beloved disciple, - "I have taken her for my own" or with Jesus Christ, "All that I have is Yours, and all that You have is mine."

Reflection

When we choose to follow God there are many people who seem to try and take us away from God's plan. It is very easy to listen to these people and take on their points of view. We have to realise that we do not follow people, we only follow God and often if we are seeking the advice of people who are caught up in the world and the brokenness of the world, the wisdom we will receive is a worldly wisdom, which is not wisdom at all, but foolishness. Many times when I have been speaking to people about what God's plan for them is, they quote what their friends or parents think. This can be a great blockage to us seeking and desiring what God wants. If we are to ask the advice of people, let us make sure that these people are people of God. But most of all let us make sure that we ask God first.

"I die the kings good servant, but God's first." (St Thomas Moore)

Resolution

Let us ask Mary to have the grace to say yes to God in all that He asks, just as she herself did.

Recite prayers for the day, *Veni Creator, Ave Maris Stella, Magnificat* (Pages 30-32)

Day 11 Renouncing the Spirit of the World

Theme: Seeking what is Important to God

Opening Prayer

Come Holy Spirit, come by means of the powerful intercession of the Immaculate Heart of Mary your well beloved spouse (3 times)

Scripture

James 1:27

Pure, unspoilt religion, in the eyes of God our Father, is this: coming to the help of orphans and widows in their hardships, and keeping oneself uncontaminated by the world.

St. Louis de Montfort Reading for today
From True Devotion (Reference #50)

Being the way by which Jesus Christ came to us the first time, Mary will also be the way by which He will come the second time, though not in the same manner.

Being the sure means and the straight and immaculate way to go to Jesus Christ, and to find Him perfectly, it is by her that the holy souls, who are to shine forth especially in sanctity, have to find our Lord. He who shall find Mary shall find life; that is, Jesus Christ, who is the Way, the Truth, and the Life. But no one can find Mary who does not seek her; and no one can seek her, who does not know her: for we cannot seek or desire an unknown object. It is necessary then, for the greater knowledge and glory of the Most Holy Trinity, that Mary should be more known than ever.

Mary must shine forth more than ever in mercy, in might, and in grace, in these latter times: in mercy, to bring back and lovingly receive the poor strayed sinners who shall be converted and shall return to the Catholic Church.

Reflection

Blessed Mother Teresa was someone who inspired me to realise that it is through giving that we receive, and the more I've learned to give, the more I've received. Having worked with the homeless, with people who are housebound and with children who are unloved and unwanted, I have received many graces and healings from the pain of my own childhood when I felt unwanted and unloved, from the pain of being in prison, as some of the housebound people who I visited seemed to be and as in some areas of my life when I felt I did not have a home. When Jesus says to us it is through giving that we receive, He is helping us to understand a way that God can fundamentally bless and heal our lives.

Peace prayer of St Francis

Lord, make me an instrument of Your peace. Where there is hatred, let me sow love; where there is injury, pardon; where there is doubt, faith; where there is despair, hope; where there is darkness, light; where there is sadness, joy.

O, Divine Master, grant that I may not so much seek to be consoled as to console; to be understood as to understand; to be loved as to love; For it is in giving that we receive; it is in pardoning that we are pardoned; it is in dying that we are born again to eternal life.

Resolution

Ask Our Lady to help us see the needs of others before our own.

Recite prayers for the day, *Veni Creator, Ave Maris Stella, Magnificat* (Pages 30-32)

Day 12 Renouncing the Spirit of the World

Theme: We are called and chosen, to be set apart from the world.

Opening Prayer

Come Holy Spirit, come by means of the powerful intercession of the Immaculate Heart of Mary your well beloved spouse (3 times)

Scripture

John 17:6-9

Jesus said, 'I have revealed your name to those whom you took from the world to give me. They were yours and you gave them to me, and they have kept your word. Now at last they have recognised that all you have given me comes from you for I have given them the teaching you gave to me, and they have indeed accepted it and know for certain that I came from you, and have believed that it was you who sent me. It is for them that I pray. I am not praying for the world but for those you have given me, because they belong to you.'

St. Louis de Montfort Reading for today
From The Love of Eternal Wisdom (Reference #98)

Eternal Wisdom, besides being the object of the eternal Father's delight, and the joy of angels, is also the source of purest joy and consolation for man who possesses him. He gives to man a relish for everything that comes from God and makes him lose his taste for things created. He enlightens his mind with the brightness of his own light and pours into his heart an indescribable joy, sweetness and peace even when he is in the midst of the most harrowing grief and suffering, as St Paul bears witness when he exclaims, "I exceedingly abound with joy in all our tribulations" (2 Cor. 7:4).

Reflection

Upon completing these 12 days we have begun our lifelong struggle to overcome the world. It is a battle we can win if we continue to fight and ask Our Lord and the Virgin Mary to sustain us. We have the help of the Choirs of angels, our guardian angels and the Archangels, plus the intercession of all the wonderful saints of heaven.

"We need saints to live in the world to sanctify the world and not to be afraid of living in the world, to taste the pure and nice things of the world, but are not of the world." (Pope Francis)

Resolution

Blessed Mother please help me to not be afraid of being the person God created me to be and ridding myself of all the lies and deceits that the world would have me believe. Help me be inspired and guided by the gifts and fruits of the Holy Spirit. Help me not to be afraid of making mistakes or falling down, knowing that the greatest attribute of God's heart is His mercy and He's a God who loves to forgive. Help me to stand up for the truth of Jesus in every situation and be a person who is firmly placed in the will of God and trusting His love.

Recite prayers for the day, *Veni Creator, Ave Maris Stella, Magnificat* (Pages 30-32)

Veni Creator

Come, O Creator Spirit blest!
And in our souls take up Your rest;
Come with Your grace and heavenly aid,
To fill the hearts which You have made.

Great Comforter! To You we cry,
O highest gift of God Most High!
O Fount of Life! O Fire of Love!
And sweet anointing from above.

You in Your many gifts are known,
The finger of God's hand we own;
The promise of the Father, Thou!
Who does the tongue with power endow.

Kindle our senses from above,
And make our hearts overflow with love;
With patience firm and virtue high,
The weakness of our flesh supply.

Drive far from us the foe we dread,
And grant us Your true peace instead;
So shall we not, with You for guide,
Turn from the path of life aside.

O may Your grace on us bestow
The Father and the Son to know,
And evermore to hold confessed
Yourself of each the Spirit blest.

All glory while the ages run
Be to the Father and the Son
Who rose from death; the same to Thee,
O Holy Ghost, eternally.

Amen.

Ave Maris Stella

Hail, bright star of ocean,
God's own Mother blest,
Ever-sinless Virgin,
Gate of heavenly rest.

Taking that sweet Ave
Which from Gabriel came,
Peace confirm within us,
Changing Eva's name.

Break the captives' chains,
Light on blindness pour,
All our ills expelling,
Every bliss implore.

Show yourself a Mother;
May The Word Divine,
Born for us your Infant,
Hear our prayers through thine.

Virgin all excelling,
Mildest of the mild,
Freed from guilt, preserve us,
Pure and undefiled.

Keep our life all spotless,
Make our way secure,
Till we find in Jesus,
Joy forevermore.

Through the highest heaven
To the Almighty Three,
Father, Son and Spirit,
One same glory be.

Amen.

Magnificat

My soul glorifies the Lord,
  my spirit rejoices in God, my Saviour.
He looks on His servant in her lowliness;
  henceforth all ages will call me blessed.

The Almighty works marvels for me.
  Holy His name!
His mercy is from age to age,
  on those who fear Him.

He puts forth His arm in strength
  and scatters the proud-hearted.
He casts the mighty from their thrones
  and raises the lowly.

He fills the starving with good things,
  sends the rich away empty.

He protects Israel, His servant,
  remembering His mercy,
the mercy promised to our fathers,
  to Abraham and his sons forever.

Glory be to the Father and to the Son
  and to the Holy Spirit,
  as it was in the beginning, is now,
  and ever shall be, world without end

Amen

DAYS 13-19
KNOWLEDGE OF SELF

St. Louis de Montfort describes the grace of self-knowledge as the 'foundation of all other' graces. Let us begin this next section with humility asking Our Lady for the grace to see ourselves as we truly are, without condemnation but with conviction to change. We need her help to live the life of grace.

With an understanding of who we truly are, comes an understanding of how much we need God. During this week we should bring to Our Lady any areas that the Holy Spirit reveals to us, in our brokenness and sinfulness and ask Our Blessed mother for the grace, through sacrifice and penance to see ourselves as God sees us, to know ourselves as God knows us and to accept and love ourselves as God accepts and loves us.

Let us not be afraid during this week of self-knowledge to take Our Blessed Mothers hand, she was given to us at the feet of the crucified and to go back into the past and face the monsters of our sins and failings.

All spiritual growth depends on our honesty with God and ourselves. It is only by the grace of God and through the gaze of Mary that we can be truly honest and have nothing to fear. To this end during this week we will pray the litany of the Holy Spirit asking the Holy Spirit to illuminate our hearts to all the areas of ourselves that we do not know.

Theme: Through baptism we have been buried with Christ so that we may be brought to life with Him.

Opening Prayer

Come Holy Spirit, come by means of the powerful intercession of the Immaculate Heart of Mary your well beloved spouse (3 times)

Scripture

Luke 18:10 -14

Jesus said, 'Two men went up to the Temple to pray, one a Pharisee, the other a tax collector. The Pharisee stood there and said this prayer to himself, "I thank you, God, that I am not grasping, unjust, adulterous like everyone else, and particularly that I am not like this tax collector here. I fast twice a week; I pay tithes on all I get." The tax collector stood some distance away, not daring even to raise his eyes to heaven; but he beat his breast and said, "God, be merciful to me, a sinner." This man, I tell you, went home again justified; the other did not. For everyone who raises himself up will be humbled, but anyone who humbles himself will be raised up.'

St. Louis de Montfort Reading for today
From True Devotion (Reference #127)

"Men," says St. Thomas, "vow in baptism to renounce the devil and all his seductions." "This vow," says St. Augustine, "is the greatest and the most indispensable of all vows." Canon Law experts say the same thing: "The vow we make at baptism is the most important of all vows." But does anyone keep this great vow? Does anyone fulfil the promises of baptism faithfully?

Is it not true that nearly all Christians prove unfaithful to the promises made to Jesus in baptism? Where does this universal failure come from, if not from man's habitual forgetfulness of the promises and responsibilities of baptism and from the fact that scarcely anyone makes a personal ratification of the contract made with God through his sponsors?

Reflection

There are many areas of our past that we are scared to look at and to see the true causes of these failures. I believe that part of the freedom that God wants us to taste in our life is self-acceptance and understanding, and the only way we can come to this freedom is by looking at our past sins with the aid of the Holy Spirit and letting him show us the cause. Sometimes this can be painful but our Blessed Mother is here to help us through this pain. The more I have opened the doors to all the areas of my life to the light of the Holy Spirit, and not being afraid to look in the darkness and dungeon like rooms, the freer I become.

St Teresa of Avila in her writings on the interior castle concludes that to not know and understand ourselves is folly but true self-knowledge is the beginnings of wisdom

Resolution

Ask Our Lady for the grace to see our sinfulness without fear or condemnation, in the light of God's mercy.

Recite prayers for the day, *Veni Creator, Ave Maris Stella, Magnificat, Litany of the Holy Spirit*
(Pages 48-52)

Theme: Learning to be thankful, we are often ungrateful for what God has done for us

Opening Prayer

Come Holy Spirit, come by means of the powerful intercession of the Immaculate Heart of Mary your well beloved spouse (3 times)

Scripture

Luke 17:11-19

Now it happened that on the way to Jerusalem He was travelling in the borderlands of Samaria and Galilee. As He entered one of the villages, ten men suffering from a virulent skin-disease came to meet Him. They stood some way off and called to Him, 'Jesus! Master! Take pity on us.' When He saw them He said, 'Go and show yourselves to the priests.' Now as they were going away they were cleansed. Finding himself cured, one of them turned back praising God at the top of his voice and threw himself prostrate at the feet of Jesus and thanked Him. The man was a Samaritan. This led Jesus to say, 'were not all ten made clean? The other nine, where are they? It seems that no one has come back to give praise to God, except this foreigner.' And He said to the man, 'Stand up and go on your way. Your faith has saved you.'

St. Louis de Montfort Reading for today
From True Devotion (Reference #255)

To thank God for the graces He has given to our Lady, her consecrated ones will frequently say the Magnificat, following the example of Blessed Marie d'Oignies and several other saints.

The Magnificat is the only prayer we have which was composed by our Lady, or rather, composed by Jesus in her, for it was He who spoke through her lips. It is the greatest offering of praise that God ever received under the law of grace. On the one hand, it is the most humble hymn of thanksgiving and, on the other; it is the most sublime and exalted. Contained in it are mysteries so great and so hidden that even the angels do not understand them

Reflection

In the book From Prison to Praise we come to understand that there is an incredible grace and power given to us when we are willing to thank and praise God for all that He gives us. Many times in our lives it is very easy and almost second nature to thank God when everything is going well, but how often do we thank God for everything? The good, the bad and the downright terrible. For when I have learned to do this in even the bad and the terrible I have always seen or felt the love and reassurance of Jesus being with me. Sometimes this can be only a little glimpse, but nonetheless He is always there, and in these times I remember His words that I am with you always even to the end of time! So let us never tire of thanking God, as we have a God who never tires of loving us.

St. Augustine says the only thing we can do that is a completely selfless act towards God is to thank Him and praise Him for His goodness.

Resolution

Ask the Blessed Virgin Mary to inspire you to praise and thank God from your heart.

Recite prayers for the day, *Veni Creator, Ave Maris Stella, Magnificat, Litany of the Holy Spirit*
(Pages 48-52)

Day 15 Knowledge of Self

Theme: Learning to live in the light and be honest with ourselves.

Opening Prayer

Come Holy Spirit, come by means of the powerful intercession of the Immaculate Heart of Mary your well beloved spouse (3 times)

Scripture

1 John 1:6-10

If we say that we share in God's life while we are living in darkness, we are lying, because we are not living the truth. But if we live in light, as He is in light, we have a share in another's life, and the blood of Jesus, His Son, cleanses us from all sin. If we say, 'We have no sin,' we are deceiving ourselves, and truth has no place in us; if we acknowledge our sins, he is trustworthy and upright, so that He will forgive our sins and will cleanse us from all evil.

St. Louis de Montfort Reading for today
From True Devotion (Reference #99-100)

I admit that to be truly devoted to Our Lady, it is not absolutely necessary to be so holy as to avoid all sin, although this is desirable. But at least it is necessary (note what I am going to say), (1) to be genuinely determined to avoid at least all mortal sin, which outrages the Mother as well as the Son; (2) to practise self-restraint in order to avoid sin; (3) to join her confraternities, say the Rosary and other prayers, fast on Saturdays, and so on.

Such means are surprisingly effective in converting even the hardened sinner. Should you be such a sinner, with one foot in the abyss, I advise you to do as I have said. But there is an essential condition. You must perform these good works solely to obtain from God, through the intercession of Our Lady, the grace to regret your sins, obtain pardon for them and overcome your evil habits, and not to live complacently in the state of sin, disregarding the warning voice of conscience, the example of Our Lord and the saints, and the teaching of the Holy Gospel.

Reflection

Often in our lives we con ourselves into not looking at the real motivations for our actions and it is only when we step back and have the honesty to invite the Holy Spirit and His wisdom into these situations that we see what our true motivation is. So let us during this week of self knowledge make a commitment of not pretending or deceiving ourselves of how easily it is to walk into occasions of sin and protecting ourselves with truth and honesty. As one priest explained if you are on a diet you should not work in a chocolate factory.

"All spiritual growth depends on honesty with ourselves and with God." (Servant of God Fr. Denis Herlihy)

Question

What sins in my life will I try and uproot with the help of God and His grace?

Resolution

Turn to the Rosary and ask Our Lady for the grace of transparency and honesty.

Recite prayers for the day, *Veni Creator, Ave Maris Stella, Magnificat, Litany of the Holy Spirit*
(Pages 48-52)

Theme: Being changed from the inside out

Opening Prayer

Come Holy Spirit, come by means of the powerful intercession of the Immaculate Heart of Mary your well beloved spouse (3 times)

Scripture

Mark 2:21-22

Jesus said, "No one sews a piece of unshrunken cloth on an old cloak; otherwise, the patch pulls away from it, the new from the old, and the tear gets worse. And nobody puts new wine into old wineskins; otherwise, the wine will burst the skins, and the wine is lost and the skins too. No! New wine into fresh skins!'

St. Louis de Montfort Reading for today
From True Devotion (Reference #78)

Our best actions are usually tainted and spoiled by the evil that is rooted in us. When pure, clear water is poured into a foul-smelling jug, or wine into an unwashed cask that previously contained another wine, the clear water and the good wine are tainted and readily acquire an unpleasant odour. In the same way when God pours into our soul, infected by original and actual sin, the heavenly waters of His grace or the delicious wines of His love, His gifts are usually spoiled and tainted by the evil sediment left in us by sin.

Reflection

I believe that it is ok to make mistakes and fall down in the pursuit of loving and serving God and often we hurt God much more by not getting up straight away from the failures in our lives and throwing ourselves into God's arms of mercy and forgiveness as the prodigal son threw himself into his father's arms. Let us never forget that when we give God permission and invite Him into our sinful nature He is the person who heals and changes us. Not my will be done, but His will be done. Jesus said of St Mary Magdalene, Those who are forgiven much, will love much.

St Therese of Lisieux said "If I woke up having committed every mortal sin it was possible to commit I would have no other recourse but to throw myself into the arms of God my loving father and it would be like a drop of water falling into a roaring volcano".

Resolution

Let us ask Our Lady for the grace to begin anew each day and never be discouraged by our failures, but to see the hope that God's call holds for us.

Recite prayers for the day, *Veni Creator, Ave Maris Stella, Magnificat, Litany of the Holy Spirit*
(Pages 48-52)

Theme: Being carriers of God's grace

Opening Prayer

Come Holy Spirit, come by means of the powerful intercession of the Immaculate Heart of Mary your well beloved spouse (3 times)

Scripture

Romans 7:18-23

'And really, I know of nothing good living in me -- in my natural self, that is -- for though the will to do what is good is in me, the power to do it is not: the good thing I want to do, I never do; the evil thing which I do not want -- that is what I do. But every time I do what I do not want to, then it is not myself acting, but the sin that lives in me.
So I find this rule: that for me, where I want to do nothing but good, evil is close at my side. In my inmost self I dearly love God's làw, but I see that acting on my body there is a different law which battles against the law in my mind.

St. Louis de Montfort Reading for today
From True Devotion (Reference #78)

It is very difficult, considering our weakness and frailty, to keep the graces and treasures we have received from God. We carry this treasure (His grace), which is worth more than heaven and earth, in fragile vessels, that is, in a corruptible body and in a weak and wavering soul which requires very little to depress and disturb it.

Reflection

There was a time in my life when I felt that I was constantly making mistakes in what I said to people. So I had this strange inspiration that if I did not speak, I could not sin. After a week of almost complete silence a good friend of mine asked me what was going on and why I wasn't my normal chatty self. I explained my strange inspiration and he told me how stupid it sounded, he then went on to say that many people I had been helping come closer to God thought I had been avoiding them because they had upset me. He said your personality is very outgoing and God uses you in that way, do not be afraid of making mistakes, be more afraid of not serving God in the way He made you. If we wait until we are perfect to serve God, we will never serve Him because we will never be perfect.

"The Glory of God is man fully alive." (St Irenaeus)

Questions

How do we treat the graces we have been given? Are they treated as the treasures they are, or do we not use them for fear of not doing it perfectly.

Resolution

Ask Our lady for the grace to be good stewards of our personality and gifts that have been bestowed upon us and not to be afraid to use them.

Recite prayers for the day, *Veni Creator, Ave Maris Stella, Magnificat, Litany of the Holy Spirit*
(Pages 48-52)

Theme: Being small in the eyes of God

Opening Prayer

Come Holy Spirit, come by means of the powerful intercession of the Immaculate Heart of Mary your well beloved spouse (3 times)

Scripture

John 2:1-11

On the third day there was a wedding at Cana in Galilee. The mother of Jesus was there, and Jesus and His disciples had also been invited. And they ran out of wine, since the wine provided for the feast had all been used, and the mother of Jesus said to Him, 'They have no wine. 'Jesus said, 'Woman, what do you want from me? My hour has not come yet. 'His mother said to the servants, 'Do whatever He tells you.' There were six stone water jars standing there, meant for the ablutions that are customary among the Jews: each could hold twenty or thirty gallons. Jesus said to the servants, 'Fill the jars with water,' and they filled them to the brim. Then He said to them, 'Draw some out now and take it to the president of the feast. They did this; the president tasted the water, and it had turned into wine. Having no idea where it came from -- though the servants who had drawn the water knew -- the president of the feast called the bridegroom and said, 'Everyone serves good wine first and the worse wine when the guests are well wined; but you have kept the best wine till now.' This was the first of Jesus' signs: it was at Cana in Galilee. He revealed His glory, and His disciples believed in Him.

St. Louis de Montfort Reading for today
From Secret of Mary (Reference #36)

In going to Jesus through Mary, we are really paying honour to Our Lord, for we are showing that, because of our sins, we are unworthy to approach His infinite holiness directly on our own.

We are showing that we need Mary, His holy Mother, to be our advocate and mediatrix with Him who is our Mediator. We are going to Jesus as Mediator and Brother, and at the same time humbling ourselves before Him who is Our God and our Judge. In short, we are practicing humility, something that always gladdens the heart of God.

Reflection

Betty Brennan who has given many talks around the world to hundreds of thousands of people says that before she speaks she gives her pride, her wanting people to love and accept her, to God and asks Him to use her in humility and smallness to glorify Him. I believe that when we give God our pride and we are willing to look at our pride, He gives us His humility and an understanding as to what it is to be humble. At the wedding feast of Cana, Jesus is humble enough to do what His mother asks Him and there is a beautiful miracle that takes place in honour of Jesus's humility and divinity. When we are obedient in humility to what God asks us we learn true freedom.

"Satan can even clothe himself in a cloak of humility, but he does not know how to wear the cloak of obedience." (Diary of St Faustina, paragraph. 939)

Resolution

Blessed Mother, please help me to have humility and obedience to God's will in my life. Help me to wear the cloak of humility and obedience as you wore it.

Recite prayers for the day, *Veni Creator, Ave Maris Stella, Magnificat, Litany of the Holy Spirit*
(Pages 48-52)

Day 19 Knowledge of Self

Theme: Dying to our own will and being alive to God's plan

Opening Prayer

Come Holy Spirit, come by means of the powerful intercession of the Immaculate Heart of Mary your well beloved spouse (3 times)

Scripture

John 12:24-25

Jesus said, " In all truth I tell you, unless a wheat grain falls into the earth and dies, it remains only a single grain; but if it dies it yields a rich harvest. Anyone who loves his life loses it; anyone who hates his life in this world will keep it for eternal life."

St. Louis de Montfort Reading for today
From True Devotion (Reference #81)

In order to empty ourselves of ourselves, we must die to ourselves daily. That is to say, we must renounce the operations of the powers of our soul, and of the senses of our body. We must see as if we saw not, understand as if we understood not, and make use of the things of this world as if we made no use of them at all. This is what St. Paul calls dying daily, if the grain of corn falling on the earth does not die; it remains earth, and brings forth no good fruit. If we die not to ourselves, and if our holiest devotions do not incline us to this necessary and useful death, we shall bring forth no fruit worth anything, and our devotions will become useless. All our works will be stained by self-love and our own will; and this will cause God to hold in abomination the greatest sacrifices we can make, and the best actions we can do; so that at our death we shall find our hands empty of virtues and of merits, and we shall not have one spark of pure love, which is only communicated to souls dead to themselves, souls whose life is hidden with Jesus Christ in God.

Reflection

I often hear people say, what do you want to do when you grow up, or have you thought about what you are going to do with your life. I believe what we should be saying is what does God want me to do with my life or how best can I seek His will. True knowledge of self helps us to understand how much we need God and knowing how much we need God helps us to understand how essential His will is in our lives. Let us live our lives according to His plan, knowing that our true happiness and freedom depends completely on this.

"Because God has made us for Himself, our hearts are restless until they rest in Him." (St Augustine)

Question

To die to oneself is not just to renounce sin but purify our hearts. This change is not possible without the cross. Where do you encounter the cross in your life? Do you embrace the cross and try to carry it faithfully or do you seek out opportunities to set it aside?

Resolution

Ask our Lady for the grace to see that in dying to ourselves we are giving up things that will not satisfy for the good things God has planned for our happiness and fulfilment.

Recite prayers for the day, *Veni Creator, Ave Maris Stella, Magnificat, Litany of the Holy Spirit*
(Pages 48-52)

As you have completed these days of knowledge of self take some time to reflect upon how sin enslaves us and keeps us from knowing the freedom we were created for. In this reflection let us look at ways to be more open to God's will and to be obedient to that will, letting go of the world's lies and embracing His truth.

Veni Creator

Come, O Creator Spirit blest!
And in our souls take up Your rest;
Come with Your grace and heavenly aid,
To fill the hearts which You have made.

Great Comforter! To You we cry,
O highest gift of God Most High!
O Fount of Life! O Fire of Love!
And sweet anointing from above.

You in Your many gifts are known,
The finger of God's hand we own;
The promise of the Father, Thou!
Who does the tongue with power endow.

Kindle our senses from above,
And make our hearts overflow with love;
With patience firm and virtue high,
The weakness of our flesh supply.

Drive far from us the foe we dread,
And grant us Your true peace instead;
So shall we not, with You for guide,
Turn from the path of life aside.

O may Your grace on us bestow
The Father and the Son to know,
And evermore to hold confessed
Yourself of each the Spirit blest.

All glory while the ages run
Be to the Father and the Son
Who rose from death; the same to Thee,
O Holy Ghost, eternally.

Amen.

Ave Maris Stella

Hail, bright star of ocean,
God's own Mother blest,
Ever-sinless Virgin,
Gate of heavenly rest.

Taking that sweet Ave
Which from Gabriel came,
Peace confirm within us,
Changing Eva's name.

Break the captives' chains,
Light on blindness pour,
All our ills expelling,
Every bliss implore.

Show yourself a Mother;
May The Word Divine,
Born for us your Infant,
Hear our prayers through thine.

Virgin all excelling,
Mildest of the mild,
Freed from guilt, preserve us,
Pure and undefiled.

Keep our life all spotless,
Make our way secure,
Till we find in Jesus,
Joy forevermore.

Through the highest heaven
To the Almighty Three,
Father, Son and Spirit,
One same glory be.

Amen.

Magnificat

My soul glorifies the Lord,
   my spirit rejoices in God, my Saviour.
He looks on His servant in her lowliness;
   henceforth all ages will call me blessed.

The Almighty works marvels for me.
   Holy His name!
His mercy is from age to age,
   on those who fear Him.

He puts forth His arm in strength
   and scatters the proud-hearted.
He casts the mighty from their thrones
   and raises the lowly.

He fills the starving with good things,
   sends the rich away empty.

He protects Israel, His servant,
   remembering His mercy,
the mercy promised to our fathers,
   to Abraham and his sons forever.

Glory be to the Father and to the Son
   and to the Holy Spirit,
   as it was in the beginning, is now,
   and ever shall be, world without end

Amen

Litany of the Holy Spirit

Lord, have mercy on us.	Lord, have mercy on us.
Christ, have mercy on us.	Christ, have mercy on us.
Lord, have mercy on us.	Lord, have mercy on us.
Father all powerful,	have mercy on us
Jesus, Eternal Son of the Father	
Redeemer of the world,	save us.
Spirit of the Father and the Son	
boundless life of both,	sanctify us.
Holy Trinity,	hear us
Holy Spirit, Who proceeds from	
The Father and the Son,	enter our hearts.
Holy Spirit, Who is equal to	
The Father and the Son,	enter our hearts.
Promise of God the Father,	have mercy on us.
Ray of heavenly light,	have mercy on us
Author of all good,	have mercy on us
Source of heavenly water,	have mercy on us
Consuming fire,	have mercy on us
Ardent charity,	have mercy on us
Spiritual unction,	have mercy on us
Spirit of love and truth,	have mercy on us
Spirit of wisdom and understanding,	have mercy on us
Spirit of counsel and fortitude,	have mercy on us
Spirit of knowledge and piety,	have mercy on us
Spirit of the fear of the Lord,	have mercy on us
Spirit of grace and prayer,	have mercy on us
Spirit of peace and meekness,	have mercy on us
Spirit of modesty and innocence,	have mercy on us
Holy Spirit, the Comforter,	have mercy on us
Holy Spirit, the Sanctifier,	have mercy on us
Holy Spirit, Who governs the Church,	have mercy on us
Gift of God, the Most High,	have mercy on us
Spirit Who fills the universe,	have mercy on us
Spirit of the adoption of the children of God,	have mercy on us

Holy Spirit,	inspire us with horror of sin.
Holy Spirit,	come and renew the face of the earth.
Holy Spirit,	shed Your light in our souls.
Holy Spirit,	engrave Your law in our hearts
Holy Spirit,	inflame us with the flame of Your love.
Holy Spirit,	open to us the treasures of Your graces
Holy Spirit,	teach us to pray well.
Holy Spirit,	enlighten us with Your heavenly inspirations.
Holy Spirit,	lead us in the way of salvation
Holy Spirit,	grant us the only necessary knowledge.
Holy Spirit,	inspire in us the practice of good.
Holy Spirit,	grant us the merits of all virtues.
Holy Spirit,	make us persevere in justice.
Holy Spirit,	be our everlasting reward.

V. Lamb of God, Who takes away the sins of the world,
R. Send us Your Holy Spirit.

V. Lamb of God, Who takes away the sins of the world,
R. Pour down into our souls the gifts of the Holy Spirit.

V. Lamb of God, Who takes away the sins of the world,
R. Grant us the Spirit of wisdom and piety.

V. Come, Holy Spirit! Fill the hearts of Your faithful,
R. And enkindle in them the fire of Your love.

Let Us Pray
Grant, O Merciful Father, that Your Divine Spirit may enlighten, inflame and purify us, that He may penetrate us with His heavenly dew and make us fruitful in good works, through Our Lord Jesus Christ, Your Son, Who with You, in the unity of the same Spirit, lives and reigns, one God, forever and ever.

Amen.

Spouse of the Spirit

Knowledge of Mary is a gift so great that it is nothing less than a privileged grace that one receives from the hand of the Almighty Himself.
St. Louis de Montfort places a great emphasis on this in speaking of Our Lady.
Mary is the supreme masterpiece of Almighty God and He has reserved the knowledge and possession of her for Himself. Mary is the sealed fountain and the faithful spouse of the Holy Spirit where only He may enter. She is the sanctuary and resting-place of the Blessed Trinity where God dwells in greater and more divine splendour than anywhere else in the universe, not excluding His dwelling above the cherubim and seraphim. No creature, however pure, may enter there without being specially privileged. (True Devotion No. 5)

Our Lady is inviting us to go deeper into a more personal and intimate relationship with her and she will lead us into the heart of Christ her Son. To that end this week we will pray the Litany of the Blessed Virgin Mary, asking for the grace of a deeper knowledge of her role.

It is recommended that you pray a rosary each day, throughout the rest of the consecration.

Theme: Our Lady is the carrier of God's grace to us

Opening Prayer

Come Holy Spirit, come by means of the powerful intercession of the Immaculate Heart of Mary your well beloved spouse (3 times)

Scripture

Revelation12:1

Now a great sign appeared in heaven: a woman, robed with the sun, standing on the moon, and on her head a crown of twelve stars.

St. Louis de Montfort Reading for today
From True Devotion (Reference #44)

Mary alone found grace before God without the help of any other creature. All those who have since found grace before God have found it only through her. She was full of grace when she was greeted by the Archangel Gabriel and was filled with grace to overflowing by the Holy Spirit when He so mysteriously overshadowed her. From day to day, from moment to moment, she increased so much this twofold plenitude that she attained an immense and inconceivable degree of grace. So much so, that the Almighty made her the sole custodian of His treasures and the sole dispenser of His graces. She can now ennoble, exalt and enrich all she chooses. She can lead them along the narrow path to heaven and guide them through the narrow gate to life. She can give a royal throne, sceptre and crown to whom she wishes. Jesus is always and everywhere the fruit and Son of Mary and Mary is everywhere the genuine tree that bears that Fruit of life, the true Mother who bears that Son.

Reflection

A priest once mentioned that he was doing quite well and had a good relationship with Jesus, then a beautiful Lady came along and showed him oceans of Jesus that he never knew existed. That Lady was Mary, our blessed Mother.

St Therese of Lisieux says there is an elevator that leads us directly to heaven, which many believe is consecrating our heart to Jesus through Mary.

Resolution

Let us ask Mary to reveal Jesus to us, and in so doing reveal herself to us.

Recite prayers for the day, *Veni Creator, Ave Maris Stella, Magnificat, Litany of the Blessed Virgin Mary, St Louis de Montfort's prayer to Mary.* (Pages 68-74)

Theme: Our Lady as our defender from evil

Opening Prayer

Come Holy Spirit, come by means of the powerful intercession of the Immaculate Heart of Mary your well beloved spouse (3 times)

Scripture

Genesis 3:10-15

But The Lord God called to the man. 'Where are you?' He asked. 'I heard the sound of you in the garden,' he replied. 'I was afraid because I was naked, so I hid. 'Who told you that you were naked?' He asked. 'Have you been eating from the tree I forbade you to eat?. The man replied, 'It was the woman you put with me; she gave me some fruit from the tree, and I ate it.' Then God said to the woman, 'Why did you do that?' The woman replied, 'The serpent tempted me and I ate.' Then God said to the serpent, 'Because you have done this, Accursed be you of all animals, wild and tame! On your belly you will go and on dust you will feed as long as you live. I shall put enmity between you and the woman, and between your offspring and hers; it will crush your head and you will strike its heel.'

St. Louis de Montfort Reading for today
From True Devotion (Reference #52)

God has established only one enmity - but it is an irreconcilable one - which will last and even go on increasing to the end of time. That enmity is between Mary, His worthy Mother, and the devil, between the children and the servants of the Blessed Virgin and the children and followers of Lucifer. Thus the most fearful enemy that God has set up against the devil is Mary, His holy Mother.

Reflection

One night a person had a dream, and in that dream there was a man who was possessed by evil spirits. Having tried everything to set this man free, the person then said three times, Come Holy Spirit, come by means of the powerful intercession of the Immaculate Heart of Mary your well beloved spouse, to which the man was completely delivered. In our everyday life there is no greater weapon against evil than the gift of Mary through the grace of God.

"When we pray the rosary we chain up the devil." (St Padre Pio)

Resolution

Ask the Blessed Virgin Mary for the grace of spiritual protection from any attacks or snares of the evil one.

Recite prayers for the day, *Veni Creator, Ave Maris Stella, Magnificat, Litany of the Blessed Virgin Mary, St Louis de Montfort's prayer to Mary.* (Pages 68-74)

Theme: Our Lady teaches us how to receive like children

Opening Prayer

Come Holy Spirit, come by means of the powerful intercession of the Immaculate Heart of Mary your well beloved spouse (3 times)

Scripture

Matthew 7:7-11

Jesus said 'Ask, and it will be given to you; search, and you will find; knock, and the door will be opened to you. Everyone who asks receives; everyone who searches finds; everyone who knocks will have the door opened. Is there anyone among you who would hand his son a stone when he asked for bread? Or would hand him a snake when he asked for a fish? If you, then, evil as you are, know how to give your children what is good, how much more will your Father in heaven give good things to those who ask him!'

St. Louis de Montfort Reading for today
Secret of Mary (Reference Numbers 11-12)

As in the natural life a child must have a father and a mother, so in the supernatural life of grace a true child of the Church must have God for his Father and Mary for his mother.

If anyone, then, wishes to become a member of Jesus Christ, and consequently be filled with grace and truth, he must be formed in Mary through the grace of Jesus Christ, which she possesses with a fullness enabling her to communicate it abundantly to true members of Jesus Christ, her true children.

Reflection

Whenever we have a problem or a situation for which we can't find a solution. If we take the time to speak it out to our blessed mother. She seems to give us the solution, take away the problem and give us her peace.

"When Mary guides you, you will feel no fatigue." (St Bernard of Clairvaux)

Resolution

Ask Our Blessed Mother to open our hearts to her and receive her peace like a child who trusts in their mother.

Recite prayers for the day, *Veni Creator, Ave Maris Stella, Magnificat, Litany of the Blessed Virgin Mary, St Louis de Montfort's prayer to Mary.*
(Pages 68-74)

Day 23 Knowledge of Mary

Theme: Through Our Lady we find a deeper union with Christ

Opening Prayer

Come Holy Spirit, come by means of the powerful intercession of the Immaculate Heart of Mary your well beloved spouse (3 times)

Scripture

Luke 2:6-7

Now it happened that, while they were there, the time came for her to have her child, and she gave birth to a son, her first-born. She wrapped Him in swaddling clothes and laid Him in a manger because there was no room for them at the inn.

St. Louis de Montfort Reading for today
From True Devotion (Reference #157)

Mary is the most perfect and the most holy of all creatures, and Jesus, who came to us in a perfect manner, chose no other road for His great and wonderful journey. The Most High, the Incomprehensible One, the Inaccessible One, He who is, deigned to come down to us poor earthly creatures who are nothing at all. How was this done? The Most High God came down to us in a perfect way through the humble Virgin Mary, without losing anything of His divinity or holiness. It is likewise through Mary that we poor creatures must ascend to almighty God in a perfect manner without having anything to fear. God the Incomprehensible, allowed Himself to be perfectly comprehended and contained by the humble Virgin Mary without losing anything of His immensity. So we must let ourselves be perfectly contained and led by the humble Virgin without any reserve on our part.

God, the Inaccessible, drew near to us and united Himself closely, perfectly and even personally to our humanity through Mary without losing anything of His majesty. So it is also through Mary that we must draw near to God and unite ourselves to Him perfectly, intimately, and without fear of being rejected. Lastly, He who is deigned to come down to us who are not and turned our nothingness into God, or He who is. He did this perfectly by giving and submitting Himself entirely to the young Virgin Mary, without ceasing to be in time He who is from all eternity. Likewise it is through Mary that we, who are nothing, may become like God by grace and glory. We accomplish this by giving ourselves to her so perfectly and so completely as to remain nothing, as far as self is concerned, and to be everything in her, without any fear of illusion.

Reflection

There was once a soul living in a religious community, who often felt very unworthy to go directly to Jesus, but had no problem praying and speaking to our blessed mother and by doing this was brought back to unity with Jesus.

"When you know Mary, you know Jesus." (Blessed Mother Teresa)

Resolution

We ask Mary to hold us in our helplessness as she held the baby Jesus in His vulnerability.

Recite prayers for the day, *Veni Creator, Ave Maris Stella, Magnificat, Litany of the Blessed Virgin Mary, St Louis de Montfort's prayer to Mary.* (Pages 68-74)

Theme: We can trust Our Lady with all we have, both material and spiritual

Opening Prayer

Come Holy Spirit, come by means of the powerful intercession of the Immaculate Heart of Mary your well beloved spouse (3 times)

Scripture

Matthew 6:19-21

Jesus said 'Do not store up treasures for yourselves on earth, where moth and woodworm destroy them and thieves can break in and steal. But store up treasures for yourselves in heaven, where neither moth nor woodworm destroys them and thieves cannot break in and steal. For wherever your treasure is, there will your heart be also.'

St. Louis de Montfort Reading for today
True devotion (reference #78)

Rejoice and be glad! Here is a secret, which I am revealing to you, a secret unknown to most Christians, even the most devout.

Do not commit the gold of your charity, the silver of your purity to a threadbare sack or a battered old chest, or the waters of heavenly grace or the wines of your merits and virtues to a tainted and fetid cask, such as you are. Otherwise you will be robbed by thieving devils that are on the lookout day and night waiting for a favourable opportunity to plunder. If you do so all those pure gifts from God will be spoiled by the unwholesome presence of self-love, inordinate self-reliance, and self-will.

Pour into the bosom and the heart of Mary all your treasures, all your graces, and all your virtues. She is a spiritual vessel, she is a vessel of honour, and she is a marvellous vessel of devotion.

Since God Himself has been shut up in person, with all His perfections, in that vessel, it has become altogether spiritual, and the spiritual abode of the most spiritual souls. It has become honourable, and the throne of honour for the grandest princes of eternity. It has become wonderful in devotion, and a dwelling the most illustrious for sweetness's, for graces, and for virtues. It has become rich as a house of gold, strong as a tower of David, and pure as a tower of ivory.

Reflection

A woman who was very worried about the lifestyle of her teenage son, who seemed to be destroying himself with drugs and drink, consecrated him one day to the Immaculate Heart of Mary. After a short time the young man was converted and became a religious brother. He was asked to give his testimony at his local church and took the picture from the family home of Mary which he had prayed to in the lead up to his conversion. On the way back from the talk he noticed that his name was written on the back of the picture and he asked his mother why this was? She said, when I consecrated you to the heart of Mary I wrote your name on the back of the picture as a sign of your consecration.

You only have to see how much God the Father trusted Mary with our salvation, Jesus as a helpless baby, to see how much we can trust Mary. (Fr. Stephen Vooght)

Questions

What are the greatest blessings you have received? What is the most prized treasure of your heart? Now have the confidence to turn all of these over to the care and custody of Our Lady

Resolution

Let us ask God for the grace to give everything to Him through Mary.

Recite prayers for the day, *Veni Creator, Ave Maris Stella, Magnificat, Litany of the Blessed Virgin Mary, St Louis de Montfort's prayer to Mary.* (Pages 68-74)

Theme: Our Lady helps us to be simple

Opening Prayer

Come Holy Spirit, come by means of the powerful intercession of the Immaculate Heart of Mary your well beloved spouse (3 times)

Scripture

Matthew 19:13-14

Then people brought little children to Him, for Him to lay His hands on them and pray. The disciples scolded them, but Jesus said, 'Let the little children alone, and do not stop them from coming to me; for it is to such as these that the kingdom of Heaven belongs.'

St. Louis de Montfort Reading for today
Secret of Mary (Reference #57)

To sum up, Mary becomes all things for the soul that wishes to serve Jesus Christ. She enlightens His mind with her pure faith. She deepens His heart with her humility. She enlarges and inflames His heart with her charity, makes it pure with her purity, makes it noble and great through her motherly care. But why dwell any longer on this? Experience alone will teach us the wonders wrought by Mary in the soul, wonders so great that the wise and the proud, and even a great number of devout people find it hard to credit them.

Reflection

A best selling author who had led a life of crime before he was converted, told how his mother wouldn't read the first half of his autobiography where he described his life as a gangster, but enjoyed reading the second half which described his growing in the wonder and love of God. On his way to meet his mother, his brother rang him and told him to be aware because their mum had read the first half of the book. This filled his heart with trepidation at what she might think. When he asked his mother what she felt about all the terrible things he had done she said, "I thought, my poor wounded little boy" and started crying.

When we see ourselves through the eyes of our Blessed Mother we are never judged or condemned, but see ourselves through the merciful loving eyes of Christ.

"When you pray to Mary you will not despair" (St Bernard)

Questions

What aspect of your spirit is most like Our Lady? Which aspect is most unlike and opposed to her?

Resolution

Let us ask our Blessed Mother to see ourselves as she sees us.

Recite prayers for the day, *Veni Creator, Ave Maris Stella, Magnificat, Litany of the Blessed Virgin Mary, St Louis de Montfort's prayer to Mary.* (Pages 68-74)

Theme: Growing closer to Our Lady leads us into discipleship of Christ

Opening Prayer

Come Holy Spirit, come by means of the powerful intercession of the Immaculate Heart of Mary your well beloved spouse (3 times)

Scripture

Matthew 10:24-25

Jesus said 'A disciple is not superior to teacher, nor slave to master. It is enough for disciple to grow to be like teacher, and slave like master.

St. Louis de Montfort Reading for today
True Devotion (Reference #219)

St. Augustine speaking to our Blessed Lady says, "You are worthy to be called the mould of God." Mary is a mould capable of forming people into the image of the God-man. Anyone who is cast into this divine mould is quickly shaped and moulded into Jesus and Jesus into him. At little cost and in a short time he will become Christ-like since he is cast into the very same mould that fashioned a God-man.

Reflection

There was a young boy whose mother couldn't love him and ended up badly mistreating him, both physically and mentally. Many years later when he was 38 years old he discovered his heavenly mother as he was praying a rosary in a prayer house. Mary revealed to him the tenderness and love that he had never experienced before at the hands of his own mother. Three days later she took him to heaven as he was baptised on his deathbed, following a sudden brain haemorrhage.

"When we take the rosary we take our Lady's hand and we are lead to where Jesus wants us to be" (St Dominic)

Questions

Do we really believe that Jesus wants the best for us in our lives, and if we do, what is stopping us giving everything to Mary and in so doing receiving the very best from Jesus?

Resolution

In our rosary let us ask Mary to reveal everything Jesus wants from us and the grace to be able to surrender all those things to him.

Recite prayers for the day, *Veni Creator, Ave Maris Stella, Magnificat, Litany of the Blessed Virgin Mary, St Louis de Montfort's prayer to Mary.* (Pages 68-74)

Veni Creator

Come, O Creator Spirit blest!
And in our souls take up Your rest;
Come with Your grace and heavenly aid,
To fill the hearts which You have made.

Great Comforter! To You we cry,
O highest gift of God Most High!
O Fount of Life! O Fire of Love!
And sweet anointing from above.

You in Your many gifts are known,
The finger of God's hand we own;
The promise of the Father, Thou!
Who does the tongue with power endow.

Kindle our senses from above,
And make our hearts overflow with love;
With patience firm and virtue high,
The weakness of our flesh supply.

Drive far from us the foe we dread,
And grant us Your true peace instead;
So shall we not, with You for guide,
Turn from the path of life aside.

O may Your grace on us bestow
The Father and the Son to know,
And evermore to hold confessed
Yourself of each the Spirit blest.

All glory while the ages run
Be to the Father and the Son
Who rose from death; the same to Thee,
O Holy Ghost, eternally.

Amen.

Ave Maris Stella

Hail, bright star of ocean,
God's own Mother blest,
Ever-sinless Virgin,
Gate of heavenly rest.

Taking that sweet Ave
Which from Gabriel came,
Peace confirm within us,
Changing Eva's name.

Break the captives' chains,
Light on blindness pour,
All our ills expelling,
Every bliss implore.

Show yourself a Mother;
May The Word Divine,
Born for us your Infant,
Hear our prayers through thine.

Virgin all excelling,
Mildest of the mild,
Freed from guilt, preserve us,
Pure and undefiled.

Keep our life all spotless,
Make our way secure,
Till we find in Jesus,
Joy forevermore.

Through the highest heaven
To the Almighty Three,
Father, Son and Spirit,
One same glory be.

Amen.

Magnificat

My soul glorifies the Lord,
  my spirit rejoices in God, my Saviour.
He looks on His servant in her lowliness;
  henceforth all ages will call me blessed.

The Almighty works marvels for me.
  Holy His name!
His mercy is from age to age,
  on those who fear Him.

He puts forth His arm in strength
  and scatters the proud-hearted.
He casts the mighty from their thrones
  and raises the lowly.

He fills the starving with good things,
  sends the rich away empty.

He protects Israel, His servant,
  remembering His mercy,
the mercy promised to our fathers,
  to Abraham and his sons forever.

Glory be to the Father and to the Son
  and to the Holy Spirit,
  as it was in the beginning, is now,
  and ever shall be, world without end

Amen

Litany of the Blessed Virgin Mary

Lord have mercy.	Lord have mercy.
Christ have mercy.	Christ have mercy.
Lord have mercy.	Lord have mercy.
Christ, hear us.	Christ, graciously hear us.
God the Father of Heaven,	have mercy on us.
God the Son, Redeemer of the world,	have mercy on us.
God the Holy Spirit,	have mercy on us.
Holy Trinity, one God,	have mercy on us
Holy Mary,	pray for us
Holy Mother of God,	pray for us
Holy Virgin of virgins,	pray for us
Mother of Christ,	pray for us
Mother of divine grace,	pray for us
Mother most pure,	pray for us
Mother most chaste,	pray for us
Mother inviolate,	pray for us
Mother undefiled,	pray for us
Mother most amiable,	pray for us
Mother most admirable,	pray for us
Mother of good counsel,	pray for us
Mother of our Creator,	pray for us
Mother of our Redeemer,	pray for us
Virgin most prudent,	pray for us
Virgin most venerable,	pray for us
Virgin most renowned,	pray for us
Virgin most powerful,	pray for us
Virgin most merciful,	pray for us
Virgin most faithful,	pray for us
Mirror of justice,	pray for us
Seat of wisdom,	pray for us
Cause of our joy,	pray for us
Spiritual vessel,	pray for us
Vessel of honour,	pray for us
Singular vessel of devotion,	pray for us
Mystical rose,	pray for us
Tower of David,	pray for us
Tower of ivory,	pray for us
House of gold,	pray for us
Ark of the covenant,	pray for us

Gate of Heaven,	pray for us
Morning Star,	pray for us
Health of the sick,	pray for us
Refuge of sinners,	pray for us
Comforter of the afflicted,	pray for us
Help of Christians,	pray for us
Queen of Angels,	pray for us
Queen of Patriarchs,	pray for us
Queen of Prophets,	pray for us
Queen of Apostles,	pray for us
Queen of Martyrs,	pray for us
Queen of Confessors,	pray for us
Queen of Virgins,	pray for us
Queen of all Saints,	pray for us
Queen conceived without original sin,	pray for us
Queen of the most holy Rosary,	pray for us
Queen of peace,	pray for us

V. Lamb of God, Who takes away the sins of the world:
R. Spare us, O Lord.

V. Lamb of God, Who takes away the sins of the world:
R. Graciously hear us, O Lord.

V. Lamb of God, Who takes away the sins of the world:
R. Have mercy on us.

V. Pray for us, most holy Mother of God,
R. That we may be made worthy of the promises of Christ.

Let us pray.

Lord God, give to your people the joy of continual health in mind and body. With the prayers of the Virgin Mary to help us, guide us through the sorrows of this life to eternal happiness in the life to come. Grant this through our Lord Jesus Christ, your Son, who lives and reigns with you and the Holy Spirit, one God, forever and ever Amen

St. Louis de Montfort's Prayer to Mary

Recommended to pray this at least once this week but, as often as you wish.

Hail Mary, beloved Daughter of the Eternal Father. Hail Mary, admirable Mother of the Son. Hail Mary, faithful Spouse of the Holy Spirit. Hail Mary, my Mother, my loving Mistress, my powerful sovereign. Hail, my joy, my glory, my heart and my soul. You are all mine by mercy, and I am yours by justice. But I am not yet sufficiently yours. I now give myself wholly to you without keeping anything back for others or myself. If you see anything in me that does not belong to you, I beseech you to take it and make yourself the absolute Mistress of all that is mine.

Destroy in me all that may displease God; root it up and bring it to nothing. Place and cultivate in me everything that is pleasing to you. May the light of your faith dispel the darkness of my mind. May your profound humility take the place of my pride; may your sublime contemplation check the distractions of my wandering imagination. May the continuous sight of God fill my memory with His Presence; may the burning love of your heart inflame the lukewarmness of mine. May your virtues take the place of my sins; may your merits be my only adornment in the sight of God and make up for all that is wanting in me. Finally, dearly beloved Mother, grant, if it be possible, that I may have no other spirit but yours to know Jesus, and His Divine Will; that I may have no other soul but yours to praise and glorify God; that I may have no other heart but yours to love God with a love as pure and ardent as yours.

I do not ask you for visions, revelations, sensible devotions, or spiritual pleasures. It is your privilege to see God clearly, it is your privilege to enjoy heavenly bliss; it is your privilege to triumph gloriously in heaven at the right hand of your Son and to hold absolute sway over angels, men, and demons.

It is your privilege to dispose of all the gifts of God, just as you will. Such, O heavenly Mary, the 'best part', which the Lord has given you, and which shall never be taken away from you – and this thought fills my heart with joy. As for my part here below, I wish for no other than that which was yours, to believe sincerely without spiritual pleasures, to suffer joyfully without human consolation, to die continually to myself without respite, and to work zealously and unselfishly for you until death, as the humblest of your servants. The only grace I beg of you, for myself, is that every moment of the day, and every moment of my life, I may say, "Amen, so be it, to all that you are doing in heaven. Amen, so be it, to all you did while on earth. Amen, so be it, to all you are doing in my soul," so that you alone may fully glorify Jesus in me for time and eternity.

Amen.

DAYS 27-33
KNOWLEDGE OF JESUS CHRIST

As we are seeking to know Jesus in a more personal and intimate way, this is the week where we enter into the person who is the beginning and end, the alpha and the omega. Having rid ourselves of all the worldly distractions that stop us realising the wonder of Jesus as our friend and saviour. Then understanding our motivations and desires through the knowledge of ourselves, and getting to grips with the essential reason for our being which is to love and understand God. We have then taken Mary's hand to lead us into the heart of her son where we can be brought to the hidden life of Jesus through the eyes of our Blessed Mother. For if we want to know The Son, let us ask His mother.

During this week we will come to know Jesus' humanity and His divinity, the humble God who comes in the form of bread so that we might draw life from Him. For when we look at Jesus we see the creator of the universe and our personal friend who knows and loves us so deeply and completely. Oh what a blessing and what a joy to know Jesus more and more and to understand His love, which is beyond all knowledge, and can only be revealed through the guidance and wisdom of the Holy Spirit and His spouse.

God the Father, open the eyes of our heart that we might know Jesus your son more fully and completely than ever before.

This week we will pray the Litany of the Sacred Heart, asking for the grace of a deeper union with Christ

Theme: Christ is the pearl of great price and without Him we are never satisfied, fulfilled or complete.

Opening Prayer

Come Holy Spirit, come by means of the powerful intercession of the Immaculate Heart of Mary your well beloved spouse (3 times)

Scripture

John 15:1-5

Jesus said 'I am the true vine, and my Father is the vinedresser. Every branch in me that bears no fruit He cuts away, and every branch that does bear fruit He prunes to make it bear even more. You are clean already, by means of the word that I have spoken to you. Remain in me, as I in you. As a branch cannot bear fruit all by itself, unless it remains part of the vine, neither can you unless you remain in me. I am the vine, you are the branches. Whoever remains in me, with me in him, bears fruit in plenty; for cut off from me you can do nothing.'

St. Louis de Montfort Reading for today
True Devotion (Reference #61)

Jesus, our Saviour, true God and true man must be the ultimate end of all our other devotions; otherwise they would be false and misleading. He is the Alpha and the Omega, the beginning and end of everything. "We labour," says St. Paul, "only to make all men perfect in Jesus Christ."

For in Him alone dwells the entire fullness of the divinity and the complete fullness of grace, virtue and perfection. In Him alone we have been blessed with every spiritual blessing; He is the only teacher from whom we must learn; the only Lord on whom we should depend; the only Head to whom we should be united and the only model that we should imitate. He is the only Physician that can heal us; the only Shepherd that can feed us; the only Way that can lead us; the only Truth that we can believe; the only Life that can animate us. He alone is everything to us and He alone can satisfy all our desires.

Reflection

There was an atheist who was in hospital, seriously ill. When an Irish Catholic nurse was speaking to him and said to him "You have had everything that the world can offer you but you have never been satisfied or fulfilled" He couldn't get these words out of his heart as he had always felt there was something missing from his life. In the last months of his life he found a personal relationship with Jesus and realised that it was this that was missing. Each one of us has a heart that is restless until it rests in the loving arms of Jesus.

There is a part of our heart that will never be satisfied or complete, no matter how rich or famous we become, until we are brought to a personal relationship with Jesus. (Saint John Paul II)

Resolution

Lord Jesus, help us to know you personally so that we might have the freedom you created us for.

Recite prayers for the day, *Veni Creator, Ave Maris Stella, Magnificat, Litany of the Sacred Heart and St Louis de Montfort's prayer to Jesus.* (Pages 91-96)

Day 28 Knowledge of Jesus Christ

Theme: In Jesus, God comes to us in His humanity

Opening Prayer

Come Holy Spirit, come by means of the powerful intercession of the Immaculate Heart of Mary your well beloved spouse (3 times)

Scripture

John 1:1-5/14-16

In the beginning was the Word: the Word was with God and the Word was God. He was with God in the beginning. Through Him all things came into being, not one thing came into being except through Him. What has come into being in Him was life, life that was the light of men; and light shines in darkness, and darkness could not overpower it. The Word was the real light that gives light to everyone; He was coming into the world. The Word became flesh, He lived among us, and we saw His glory, the glory that He has from the Father as only Son of the Father, full of grace and truth. Indeed, from His fullness we have, all of us, received -- one gift replacing another.

St. Louis de Montfort Reading for today
From Secret of the Rosary (Reference #72)

During her whole life, our Saviour's holy Mother was occupied in meditating on the virtues and the sufferings of her Son. When she heard the angels sing their hymn of joy at His birth and saw the shepherds adore Him in the stable, her heart was filled with wonder and she meditated on all these marvels.

She compared the greatness of the Word incarnate to the way He humbled Himself in this lowly fashion; the straw of the crib, to His throne in the heart of His Father; the might of God, to the weakness of a his simplicity.

Reflection

A man who had just been converted who was filled with the Holy Spirit and wanted to evangelise said to his parish priest "We need to go out and tell everyone about Jesus" and the parish priest said "I have a curate who is a great preacher, and when he preaches many people come to know Jesus, and at the moment he is doing the washing up, then he is going to hoover the front room and tidy up the house. Know that Jesus is in the ordinary every day things as well as the extraordinary" Jesus is in our humanity as He reveals His humanity.

Jesus is in the pots and pans of everyday life. (St Teresa of Avila)

Resolution

Jesus, help us to understand that you are interested in the hidden small things of our life and help us to be honest and real with you.

Recite prayers for the day, *Veni Creator, Ave Maris Stella, Magnificat, Litany of the Sacred Heart, St Louis de Montfort's prayer to Jesus.*
(Pages 91-96)

Theme: We cannot have humility without obedience

Opening Prayer

Come Holy Spirit, come by means of the powerful intercession of the Immaculate Heart of Mary your well beloved spouse (3 times)

Scripture: Luke 2:41-52

Every year Jesus' parents went to Jerusalem for the Festival of the Passover. When He was twelve years old, they went up to the festival, according to the custom. After the festival was over, while His parents were returning home, the boy Jesus stayed behind in Jerusalem, but they were unaware of it. Thinking He was in their company, they travelled on for a day. Then they began looking for Him among their relatives and friends. When they did not find Him, they went back to Jerusalem to look for Him. After three days they found Him in the temple courts, sitting among the teachers, listening to them and asking them questions. Everyone who heard Him was amazed at His understanding and His answers. When His parents saw Him, they were astonished. His mother said to Him, "Son, why have you treated us like this? Your father and I have been anxiously searching for you."

"Why were you searching for me?" He asked. "Didn't you know I had to be in my Father's house?" But they did not understand what He was saying to them.

Then He went down to Nazareth with them and was obedient to them. But His mother treasured all these things in her heart. And Jesus grew in wisdom and stature, and in favour with God and man.

St. Louis de Montfort Reading for today
From True Devotion (Reference #139)

Our good Master stooped to enclose Himself in the womb of the Blessed Virgin, a captive but loving slave, and to make Himself subject to her for thirty years. As I said earlier, the human mind is bewildered when it reflects seriously upon this conduct of Incarnate Wisdom. He did not choose to give Himself in a direct manner to the human race though He could easily have done so. He chose to come through the Virgin Mary.

Thus He did not come into the world independently of others in the flower of His manhood, but He came as a frail little child dependent on the care and attention of His Mother. Consumed with the desire to give glory to God, His Father, and save the human race, He saw no better or shorter way to do so than by submitting completely to Mary.

He did this not just for the first eight, ten or fifteen years of His life like other children, but for thirty years. He gave more glory to God, His Father, during all those years of submission and dependence than He would have given by spending them working miracles, preaching far and wide, and converting all mankind. Otherwise He would have done all these things.

What immeasurable glory then do we give to God when, following the example of Jesus, we submit to Mary! With such a convincing and well-known example before us, can we be so foolish as to believe that there is a better and shorter way of giving God glory than by submitting ourselves to Mary, as Jesus did?

Reflection

A person who was in a religious community was struggling with the people who God had put in charge of him, and on one occasion was sharing with someone how weak and broken his superiors were. The person listened very attentively to his story, and then said to him "what do they think of you?" It is very easy for us to work out all the reasons why we shouldn't be obedient instead of showing the humility of Jesus who was obedient even unto death.

"Obedience is infallible when it is not contrary to morality" (Blessed Mother Teresa)

Question

How obedient am I? Am I willing to follow and learn from Mary as Jesus did?

Resolution

Lord Jesus help us to have the humility and obedience that you have showed us through your witness.

Recite prayers for the day, *Veni Creator, Ave Maris Stella, Magnificat, Litany of the Sacred Heart, St Louis de Montfort's prayer to Jesus.*

(Pages 91-96)

Theme: Take up your cross and follow me

Opening Prayer

Come Holy Spirit, come by means of the powerful intercession of the Immaculate Heart of Mary your well beloved spouse (3 times)

Scripture

Matthew 27:38-44

The passers-by jeered at Jesus, they shook their heads and said, 'So you would destroy the Temple and in three days rebuild it! Then save yourself if you are God's son and come down from the cross! The chief priests with the scribes and elders mocked Him in the same way, with the words, 'He saved others; He cannot save Himself. He is the king of Israel; let Him come down from the cross now, and we will believe in Him'.

St. Louis de Montfort Reading for today
From Love of Eternal Wisdom (Reference #169)

Incarnate Wisdom loved the cross from His infancy. (Wis 8.2) At His coming into the world, while in His Mother's womb, He received it from His eternal Father. He placed it deep in His heart, there to dominate His life, saying, "My God and my Father, I chose this cross when I was in your bosom. (Ps 39.9) I choose it now in the womb of my Mother. I love it with all my strength and I place it deep in my heart to be my spouse and my mistress."

Reflection

During his prayers a pilgrim was complaining to Jesus about his cross being too heavy and burdensome. Jesus appeared to him and showed him a door, as he opened this door the room was filled with different sized crosses. Jesus said, "Take your pick", the pilgrim selected his ideal cross and went on his way. As the pilgrim examined his cross again he realised that he had chosen the exact same cross he had been complaining about. God never gives us a burden that is too heavy for us to carry, because it is with His help and grace that we carry that burden.

"Behold the cross of the Lord, when all adversity surrounds you, rejoice for the Lion of Judah has conquered!"   (St Anthony of Padua)

Resolution

Lord Jesus, help us to carry our crosses in life, as you carried our crosses to your death.

Recite prayers for the day, *Veni Creator, Ave Maris Stella, Magnificat, Litany of the Sacred Heart, St Louis de Montfort's prayer to Jesus.*
(Pages 91-96)

Theme: No one can have greater love than to lay down his life for his friends.

Opening Prayer

Come Holy Spirit, come by means of the powerful intercession of the Immaculate Heart of Mary your well beloved spouse (3 times)

Scripture

John 15:13-15

Jesus said, 'I have loved you just as the Father has loved me. Remain in my love. If you keep my commandments you will remain in my love, just as I have kept my Father's commandments and remain in His love. I have told you this so that my own joy may be in you and your joy be complete. This is my commandment: love one another, as I have loved you. No one can have greater love than to lay down his life for his friends.'

St. Louis de Montfort Reading for today
From Friends of the Cross (Reference #57)

The Holy Spirit tells us, through the Apostles, to contemplate the crucified Christ. He bids us arm ourselves with this thought, for it is the most powerful and formidable weapon against our enemies. When you are assailed by poverty, disrepute, sorrow, temptation, and other crosses, arm yourselves with the shield, breastplate, helmet and two-edged sword, which is the remembrance of Christ crucified. It is there you will find the solution of every problem and the means to conquer all your enemies.

Reflection

Many people look at the cross and see their salvation, but do not see the humble figure of Mary with her hand outstretched to us, asking us to take her hand and journey through that crucifixion to the resurrection that Christ's death brought each one of us. A person who was very impressed with a woman who was filled with the grace of God said to her "I want your peace" she replied "Are you willing to be crucified to receive it?"

"The devil's greatest tactic is to hide the true meaning of the cross from us." (Archbishop Fulton Sheen)

Resolution

Mary, Help us take you by the hand and lead us through the crucifixion where we will find the freedom that Christ's death brought each one of us.

Recite prayers for the day, *Veni Creator, Ave Maris Stella, Magnificat, Litany of the Sacred Heart, St Louis de Montfort's prayer to Jesus.*
(Pages 91-96)

Theme: The Blessed Sacrament is the source and summit of our faith.

Opening Prayer

Come Holy Spirit, come by means of the Immaculate Heart of Mary your well beloved spouse (3 times)

Scripture

Luke 22:19-20

Then Jesus took bread, and when He had given thanks, He broke it and gave it to them, saying, 'This is my body given for you; do this in remembrance of me.' He did the same with the cup after supper, and said, 'This cup is the new covenant in my blood poured out for you.'

St. Louis de Montfort Reading for today
From Love of Eternal Wisdom (Reference #71)

Eternal Wisdom, on the one hand, wished to prove His love for man by dying in his place in order to save him, but on the other hand, He could not bear the thought of leaving him. So He devised a marvellous way of dying and living at the same time, and of abiding with man until the end of time. So, in order fully to satisfy his love, He instituted the sacrament of Holy Eucharist and went to the extent of changing and overturning nature itself.

He does not conceal Himself under a sparkling diamond or some other precious stone, because He does not want to abide with man in an ostentatious manner. But He hides Himself under the appearance of a small piece of bread - man's ordinary nourishment - so that when received He might enter the heart of man and there take His delight. Ardenter amantium hoc est - Those who love ardently act in this way. "O eternal Wisdom," says a saint, "O God who is truly lavish with Himself in His desire to be with man."

Reflection

A famous author whose son wrote to him explaining how he was feeling hopelessness and despair and feared he was losing his faith had the reply from his father "If there is one thing to put in the centre of your life that you will always have fulfilment and deep faith in God, it is the Eucharist". When we start going to Mass daily and spending time with Jesus in the blessed Sacrament in adoration our lives are transformed, for we place ourselves in the miracles of our humble God who comes in the form of bread that we may draw life from Him.

"All my strength comes from one source, Jesus in the Eucharist." (Blessed Mother Teresa)

"It would be easier for the earth to exist without the sun than without the Holy Mass" (St Padre Pio)

Resolution

Lord Jesus, give me eyes that I might see the glory of you made present in the form of bread

Recite prayers for the day, *Veni Creator, Ave Maris Stella, Magnificat, Litany of the Sacred Heart, St Louis de Montfort's prayer to Jesus.* (Pages 91-96)

Theme: To know Jesus is to serve Him and to do His will

Opening Prayer

Come Holy Spirit, come by means of the powerful intercession of the Immaculate Heart of Mary your well beloved spouse (3 times)

Scripture

Mark 16:14-18

Last of all, Jesus appeared to the eleven disciples as they were eating. He scolded them, because they did not have faith and because they were too stubborn to believe those who had seen Him alive. He said to them, "Go throughout the whole world and preach the gospel to all people. Whoever believes and is baptized will be saved; whoever does not believe will be condemned. Believers will be given the power to perform miracles: they will drive out demons in my name; they will speak in strange tongues; if they pick up snakes or drink any poison, they will not be harmed; they will place their hands on sick people, and these will get well."

St. Louis de Montfort Reading for today
From True Devotion (Reference #56-59)

But what will they be like, these servants, these slaves, these children of Mary?

They will be ministers of the Lord who, like a flaming fire, will enkindle everywhere the fires of divine love. They will become, in Mary's powerful hands, like sharp arrows, with which she will transfix her enemies.

They will be as the children of Levi, thoroughly purified by the fire of great tribulations and closely joined to God. They will carry the gold of love in their heart, the frankincense of prayer in their mind and the myrrh of mortification in their body. They will bring to the poor and lowly everywhere the sweet fragrance of Jesus, but they will bring the odour of death to the great, the rich and the proud of this world.

They will be like thunderclouds flying through the air at the slightest breath of the Holy Spirit. Attached to nothing, surprised at nothing, troubled at nothing, they will shower down the rain of God's word and of eternal life. They will thunder against sin, they will storm against the world, they will strike down the devil and his followers and for life and for death, they will pierce through and through with the two-edged sword of God's word all those against whom they are sent by Almighty God.

They will be true apostles of the latter times to whom the Lord of Hosts will give eloquence and strength to work wonders and carry off glorious spoils from His enemies. They will sleep without gold or silver and, more important still, without concern in the midst of other priests, ecclesiastics and clerics. Yet they will have the silver wings of the dove enabling them to go wherever the Holy Spirit calls them, filled as they are with the resolve to seek the glory of God and the salvation of souls. Wherever they preach, they will leave behind them nothing but the gold of love, which is the fulfilment of the whole law.

Lastly, we know they will be true disciples of Jesus Christ, imitating His poverty, His humility, His contempt of the world and His love. They will point out the narrow way to God in pure truth according to the holy Gospel, and not according to the maxims of the world. Their hearts will not be troubled, nor will they show favour to anyone; they will not spare or heed or fear any man, however powerful he may be. They will have the two-edged sword of the word of God in their mouths and the bloodstained standard of the Cross on their shoulders. They will carry the crucifix in their right hand and the rosary in their left, and the holy names of Jesus and Mary on their heart. The simplicity and self-sacrifice of Jesus will be reflected in their whole behaviour.

Such are the great men who are to come. By the will of God Mary is to prepare them to extend His rule over the impious and unbelievers. But when and how will this come about? Only God knows. For our part we must yearn and wait for it in silence and in prayer: "I have waited and waited."

Reflection

When we consecrate our heart to Jesus through Mary, we take on a role, which is to bring the love of Christ to all who we meet. We step out in faith with a resolute commitment to bring others to a deep knowledge of the role of Mary and an understanding of everyone's need of Jesus. Let us not be afraid to stand up for Christ in all that we do and all we are, through the way we live and the way we speak, bringing His truth to a world that is in desperate need of it. A wise old man once asked a young boy, "what is the most important thing in Life?" the young boy replied "You are much older and wiser than me, what is it?" The old man said "To bring as many souls to God as possible and your own first!"

"Do not be afraid to proclaim the Gospel from the rooftops!"
(Saint John Paul II)

Resolution

Let us ask our Blessed Mother to make a resolution and a promise that we will try to be fearless witnesses of the light of Christ, through going to confession regularly, receiving Jesus in the Blessed Sacrament as often as possible, by praying the rosary daily and receiving all the graces we need to truly serve her son Jesus Christ, our Lord and God by being obedient to His will.

Recite prayers for the day, *Veni Creator, Ave Maris Stella, Magnificat, Litany of the Sacred Heart, St Louis de Montfort's prayer to Jesus.*
(Pages 91-96)

Veni Creator

Come, O Creator Spirit blest!
And in our souls take up Your rest;
Come with Your grace and heavenly aid,
To fill the hearts which You have made.

Great Comforter! To You we cry,
O highest gift of God Most High!
O Fount of Life! O Fire of Love!
And sweet anointing from above.

You in Your many gifts are known,
The finger of God's hand we own;
The promise of the Father, Thou!
Who does the tongue with power endow.

Kindle our senses from above,
And make our hearts overflow with love;
With patience firm and virtue high,
The weakness of our flesh supply.

Drive far from us the foe we dread,
And grant us Your true peace instead;
So shall we not, with You for guide,
Turn from the path of life aside.

O may Your grace on us bestow
The Father and the Son to know,
And evermore to hold confessed
Yourself of each the Spirit blest.

All glory while the ages run
Be to the Father and the Son
Who rose from death; the same to Thee,
O Holy Ghost, eternally.

Amen.

Ave Maris Stella

Hail, bright star of ocean,
God's own Mother blest,
Ever-sinless Virgin,
Gate of heavenly rest.

Taking that sweet Ave
Which from Gabriel came,
Peace confirm within us,
Changing Eva's name.

Break the captives' chains,
Light on blindness pour,
All our ills expelling,
Every bliss implore.

Show yourself a Mother;
May The Word Divine,
Born for us your Infant,
Hear our prayers through thine.

Virgin all excelling,
Mildest of the mild,
Freed from guilt, preserve us,
Pure and undefiled.

Keep our life all spotless,
Make our way secure,
Till we find in Jesus,
Joy forevermore.

Through the highest heaven
To the Almighty Three,
Father, Son and Spirit,
One same glory be.

Amen.

Magnificat

My soul glorifies the Lord,
my spirit rejoices in God, my Saviour.
He looks on His servant in her lowliness;
henceforth all ages will call me blessed.

The Almighty works marvels for me.
Holy His name!
His mercy is from age to age,
on those who fear Him.

He puts forth His arm in strength
and scatters the proud-hearted.
He casts the mighty from their thrones
and raises the lowly.

He fills the starving with good things,
sends the rich away empty.

He protects Israel, His servant,
remembering His mercy,
the mercy promised to our fathers,
to Abraham and his sons forever.

Glory be to the Father and to the Son
and to the Holy Spirit,
as it was in the beginning, is now,
and ever shall be, world without end

Amen

Litany of the Sacred Heart

Lord, have mercy	Lord, have mercy
Christ, have mercy	Christ, have mercy
Lord, have mercy	Lord, have mercy
Christ, hear us	Christ, hear us
Christ, graciously hear us.	Christ, graciously hear us.

God the Father of Heaven,	have mercy on us.
God the Son, Redeemer of the world,	have mercy on us.
God, the Holy Spirit,	have mercy on us.
Holy Trinity, One God,	have mercy on us.
Heart of Jesus, Son of the Eternal Father,	have mercy on us.
Heart of Jesus, formed by the Holy Spirit in the womb of the Virgin Mother,	have mercy on us.
Heart of Jesus, substantially united to the Word of God,	have mercy on us.
Heart of Jesus, of Infinite Majesty,	have mercy on us.
Heart of Jesus, Sacred Temple of God,	have mercy on us.
Heart of Jesus, Tabernacle of the Most High,	have mercy on us.
Heart of Jesus, House of God and Gate of Heaven,	have mercy on us.
Heart of Jesus, burning furnace of charity,	have mercy on us.
Heart of Jesus, abode of justice and love,	have mercy on us.
Heart of Jesus, full of goodness and love,	have mercy on us.
Heart of Jesus, abyss of all virtues,	have mercy on us.
Heart of Jesus, most worthy of all praise,	have mercy on us.
Heart of Jesus, king and centre of all hearts,	have mercy on us.
Heart of Jesus, in whom are all treasures of wisdom and knowledge,	have mercy on us.
Heart of Jesus, in whom dwells the fullness of divinity,	have mercy on us.
Heart of Jesus, in whom the Father was well pleased,	have mercy on us.
Heart of Jesus, of whose fullness we have all received,	have mercy on us.
Heart of Jesus, desire of the everlasting hills,	have mercy on us.
Heart of Jesus, patient and most merciful,	have mercy on us.

Heart of Jesus, enriching all who invoke You,	have mercy on us.
Heart of Jesus, fountain of life and holiness,	have mercy on us.
Heart of Jesus, propitiation for our sins,	have mercy on us.
Heart of Jesus, loaded down with opprobrium,	have mercy on us.
Heart of Jesus, bruised for our offenses,	have mercy on us.
Heart of Jesus, obedient to death,	have mercy on us.
Heart of Jesus, pierced with a lance,	have mercy on us.
Heart of Jesus, source of all consolation,	have mercy on us.
Heart of Jesus, our life and resurrection,	have mercy on us.
Heart of Jesus, our peace and our reconciliation,	have mercy on us.
Heart of Jesus, victim for our sins,	have mercy on us.
Heart of Jesus, salvation of those who trust in You,	have mercy on us.
Heart of Jesus, hope of those who die in You,	have mercy on us.
Heart of Jesus, delight of all the Saints,	have mercy on us.
Lamb of God, who takes away the sins of the world,	have mercy on us.
Lamb of God, who takes away the sins of the world,	have mercy on us.
Lamb of God, who takes away the sins of the world,	have mercy on us.

V. Jesus, meek and humble of heart.
R. Make our hearts like unto Yours.

Let us pray;

Almighty and eternal God, look upon the Heart of Your most beloved Son and upon the praises and satisfaction that He offers You in the name of sinners; and to those who implore Your mercy. In Your great goodness, grant forgiveness in the name of the same Jesus Christ, Your Son, who lives and reigns with You and the Holy Spirit now and forever. Amen.

St. Louis de Montfort's Prayer to Jesus

O most loving Jesus, allow me pour out my gratitude before you, for the grace you have bestowed upon me in giving me to your holy Mother through the devotion of Holy slavery, that she may be my advocate in the presence of your majesty and my support in my extreme misery. Alas, O Lord! I am so wretched that without this dear Mother I should be certainly lost. Yes, Mary is necessary for me at Your side and everywhere: that she may appease Your just wrath, because I have so often offended You; that she may save me from the eternal punishment of Your justice, which I deserve; that she may contemplate You, speak to You, pray to You, approach You and please You; that she may help me to save my soul and the souls of others; in short, Mary is necessary for me that I may always do Your holy will and seek Your greater glory in all things. Ah, would that I could proclaim throughout the whole world the mercy that You have shown to me! Would that everyone might know I should be already damned, were it not for Mary! Would that I might offer worthy thanksgiving for so great a blessing! Mary is in me. Oh, what a treasure! Oh, what a consolation! And shall I not be entirely hers'? Oh, what ingratitude! My dear Saviour, send me death rather than such a calamity, for I would rather die than live without belonging entirely to Mary. With St. John the Evangelist at the foot of the Cross, I have taken her a thousand times for my own and as many times have given myself to her; but if I have not yet done it as You, dear Jesus, would wish, I now renew this offering as You desire me to renew it. And if You see in my soul or my body anything that does not belong to this august princess, I pray You to take it and cast it far from me, for whatever in me does not belong to Mary is unworthy of You.

O Holy Spirit, grant me all these graces. Plant in my soul the Tree of true Life, which is Mary; cultivate it and tend it so that it may grow and blossom and bring forth the fruit of life in abundance. O Holy Spirit, give me great devotion to Mary, Your faithful spouse; give me great confidence in her maternal heart and an abiding refuge in her mercy, so that by her You may truly form in me Jesus Christ, great and mighty, unto the fullness of His perfect age. Amen.

DAY OF CONSECRATION

INSTRUCTIONS FOR CONSECRATION

On the day of consecration, either fast, give alms, or offer a votive candle for the good of another (or all of the above); do some spiritual penance and approach the consecration in the spirit of mortification.

Now go to Confession (or, if that is not possible, try to go within a week) and then receive Communion with the intention of giving yourself to Jesus, as a slave of love, by the hands of Mary.

Now pray the words of the consecration on the next two pages. Copy them and have them with you at church, read them after the Mass, and sign your copy of the Act of Consecration.

Every year at least, on the same date, we should renew the consecration following the same exercises. We might also renew it every month or even every day by saying this short prayer: "I am all yours and all I have is yours, O dear Jesus, through Mary, Your holy Mother."

Consecration to Jesus through Mary

O Eternal and incarnate Wisdom! O sweetest and most adorable Jesus! True God and true man, only Son of the Eternal Father, and of Mary, always virgin! I adore You profoundly in the bosom and splendours of Your Father during eternity; and I adore You also in the virginal bosom of Mary, Your most worthy Mother, in the time of Your incarnation.

I give You thanks for You have annihilated Yourself, taking the form of a slave in order to rescue me from the cruel slavery of the devil. I praise and glorify You for You have been pleased to submit Yourself to Mary, Your holy Mother, in all things, in order to make me Your faithful slave through her. But, alas! Ungrateful and faithless as I have been, I have not kept the promises which I made so solemnly to You in my Baptism; I have not fulfilled my obligations; I do not deserve to be called Your child, or even Your slave; and as there is nothing in me which does not merit Your anger and Your repulse, I dare not come by myself before Your most holy and august Majesty. It is on this account that I have recourse to the intercession of Your most holy Mother, whom You have given me for a mediatrix with You. It is through her that I hope to obtain from You contrition, the pardon of my sins, and the acquisition and preservation of wisdom.

Hail, then, O immaculate Mary, living tabernacle of the Divinity, where the Eternal Wisdom willed to be hidden and to be adored by angels and by men! Hail, O Queen of Heaven and earth, to whose empire everything is subject which is under God. Hail, O sure refuge of sinners, whose mercy fails no one. Hear the desires which I have of the Divine Wisdom; and for that end receive the vows and offerings which in my lowliness I present to you.

I, _____, a faithless sinner, renew and ratify today in your hands the vows of my Baptism; I renounce forever Satan, his works and empty promises; and I give myself entirely to Jesus Christ, the Incarnate Wisdom, to carry my cross after Him all the days of my life, and to be more faithful to Him than I have ever been before. In the presence of all the heavenly court I choose you this day for my Mother and Mistress. I deliver and consecrate to you, as your slave, my body and soul, my goods, both interior and exterior, and even the value of all my good actions, past, present and future; leaving to you the entire and full right of disposing of me, and all that belongs to me, without exception, according to your good pleasure, for the greater glory of God in time and in eternity.

Receive, O compassionate Virgin, this little offering of my slavery, in honour of, and in union with, that subjection which the Eternal Wisdom deigned to have to your maternity; in homage to the power which both of you have over this poor sinner, and in thanksgiving for the privileges with which the Holy Trinity has favoured you. I declare that I wish henceforth, as your true slave, to seek your honour and to obey you in all things.

O admirable Mother, present me to your dear Son as His eternal slave, so that as He has redeemed me by you, by you He may receive me! O Mother of mercy, grant me the grace to obtain the true Wisdom of God; and for that end receive me among those who you love and teach, who you lead, nourish and protect as your children and your slaves.

O faithful Virgin, make me in all things so perfect a disciple, imitator and slave of the Incarnate Wisdom, Jesus Christ Your Son, that I may attain, by your intercession and by your example, to the fullness of His age on earth and of His glory in Heaven. Amen.

Sign _____

Date _____